100 Things To See On

Australia's Coral Coast

+ Karijini and the Pilbara

Exploring Eden Media

CONTENTS

INTRODUCTION

If you ask anyone who's spent time on the Coral Coast or Pilbara to share what they love so much about these regions, you'll find three common answers: nature, adventure, freedom.

Just two hour's drive north of Perth is the beginning of this world-class wilderness area that remains, quite amazingly, largely unknown to the rest of the world. Here in this sparsely populated region, it's perfectly normal to have a beach all to yourself or to free camp seaside on a patch of dirt that would be crammed with swanky resorts or million-dollar mansions anywhere else. Close encounters with wild animals are a regular experience, and at night the stars shine so bright, you'll be spotting constellations faster than you can say 'download that star app!'

The name 'Coral Coast' can be misleading, as it fails to acknowledge the bounty of experiences you can have beyond the turquoise sea. Yes, the world's largest fringing reef, Ningaloo, is the ultimate show stealer with its most famous visitor, the whale shark luring thousands of visitors each autumn and winter. But, as is often the case, it's the sideshows that sometimes steal the spotlight. Stories of orca pods hunting baby humpbacks or giant manta rays dancing around snorkellers are shared around the campfire after a whale shark day trip. Unique encounters with rock wallabies hiding in cliffs or an emu escorting chicks across the road will make you feel like you're inside a David Attenborough documentary, minus the raspy voiceover.

Beyond the ocean, there are sweeping canyons, waterholes and hot pools, ancient indigenous relics and roads that seemingly stretch to the end of the earth. And if the region wasn't magnificent enough with its primitive and raw beauty, during wildflower season, the vast plains and canyons burst forth with billions of flowers, brilliant in colour and all swaying together in the breeze.

Here is a place to push your limits and to feel alive while simultaneously slowing down to the relaxed rhythm of outback Western Australia. Whether you're catching a fish, spotting for turtles beneath your surfboard, playing hide and seek in the Pinnacles or simply soaking in the sunshine, you'll feel invigorated by every day spent here. And when the sun goes down, you'll be spoiled by a multitude of places to rest your head, from seaside campsites to luxe glamping tents, all beneath a blanket of a million stars.

You can fly in for a quick trip or join the annual winter caravan migration north, stopping at every cheap or free camp that lures you in for a day or ten. If you've brought your boat (or hired one), you can head out and explore the hundreds of islands scattered along this coastline, each one bursting with marine life and an opportunity to stock up the esky with the day's catch. And when your skin and hair is so salty that it feels like it could snap off, the icy freshwater swimming holes of Karijini and the Pilbara beckon, only half a day's drive inland. For a soul-enriching encounter in nature and a feeling of freedom away from the crowds, you're sure to find yourself on the ultimate adventure here on Australia's Coral Coast.

TRAVELLING THE CORAL COAST

GETTING TO THE CORAL COAST

BY AIR

Capital city Perth welcomes the bulk of Western Australia's domestic and international flights, and it is well connected with daily flights to all major Australian cities. The country's fourth busiest airport is also conveniently located 15km west of the CBD (that's a $35-40 taxi ride). From late 2021, a new airport link rail line will get you from Perth Airport to the CBD in less than 20 minutes.

Flying on from Perth, northbound flights reach Geraldton, Monkey Mia (Shark Bay), Carnarvon, Exmouth, Onslow and Karratha, where you can pick up a rental car or a campervan and hit the road to explore. Bear in mind that many of these airports, especially those in the north, exist to service the fly-in, fly-out mining industry, so seats are often limited and usually expensive, and then finding a hire car might be difficult.

BY ROAD

The best way to explore the Coral Coast is by road. Setting out from Perth, expect to clock up around 2000km before you close this guidebook in Karratha, allowing for a highly recommended detour inland to the Pilbara's Karijini National Park. Leapfrogging between incredible natural havens means plenty of long, lonely highway runs too, but this coastline screams 'road trip', and you can access just about all of it with a conventional, 2WD vehicle.

However, if your vehicle is a 4WD, your adventures will lead you far beyond the popular hotspots to discover quiet

coves and beaches, breezy camps, and fishing spots that are all your own. Setting out from the Perth CBD, it's a 90-minute drive (125km) to Lancelin via the uber-scenic Indian Ocean Drive, where the real exploring begins. If starting from Broome or the Kimberley, follow the Great Northern Highway south to Karratha, fuelling up at the iconic Sandfire Roadhouse en route.

WHEN TO VISIT

It's not just the landscape that changes as you travel this vast coastline; the climate does too, shifting slowly from temperate (think mild and Mediterranean) to hot and semi-arid once you cross the Tropic of Capricorn just south of Coral Bay.

Regardless of where you are headed, the dry winter months are by far the best time to travel here. Cool, comfortable temperatures prevail north of Perth from April through September when the sea is calmer following summer's cyclone season, and whales begin to migrate along the coast. Everything you can do in the water – boating, surfing, fishing, paddling and snorkelling – is pretty perfect over the winter months. Between late July and October, after a brief flurry of wintertime rain, the bloom of vibrant wildflowers that famously carpet the countryside in vivid, colourful scenes is triggered. If you can be here then, every view is spectacular.

Out of season, from October to March, you can expect far fewer crowds and hot, balmy conditions. But don't be put off if your timing lands you here over summer because that's when the Fremantle Doctor calls, cooling the coastline with soothing, onshore afternoon winds, so named because in Perth, the wind appears to come from Fremantle. Popular national parks and coastal towns bustle with local explorers over the April and July school holidays, when savvy travellers steer clear or book their accommodation and tours well in advance.

WHERE TO STAY

Anyone who can travel self-sufficiently will experience the Coral Coast and Pilbara at their very best. Whether you roll out a swag, hit the road in a campervan or tow everything you need in a caravan, with your own beds on board, you can set your own itinerary and utilise dozens of free and low-cost camping destinations waiting for you right along the coast.

Most provide stellar waterfront views, excellent facilities, and some, like the free camps at Cliff Head on the Indian Ocean Drive, sit on chunks of what would be million-dollar real estate anywhere else in the world. Every destination along this Coral Coast has at least one exceptional waterfront camp (don't miss Geraldton's Ellendale Pool camp or the beach campsites at Dirk Hartog Island).

The West Coast's working sheep stations offer more, with rare access to Indigenous and pioneer-era heritage sites, world-class surf breaks, nesting turtles and incredible fishing grounds. Spots like Warroora Station, for example, allow you to camp right on the sand, mere metres from a turquoise sea and coral reefs.

Then there's the string of big-ticket national parks that make this coastline famous, expertly catering to campers. Stretch your itinerary to allow for lengthy stays at Cape Range National Park (for beachfront camps on Australia's largest, fringing coral reef), Shark Bay's Francois Peron, Karijini's incredible gorges and lesser-known Millstream-Chichester National Park for bike riding and hiking.

WHAT TO PACK

Whatever the time of year, you'll need a wardrobe of lightweight, breathable clothing to protect from the sun and heat. Over the peak winter months, add a set of warm clothes for travels close to Perth and early morning adventures inland to explore the wildflowers. Pack swimmers, hats, reef-friendly sunscreen, natural insect repellent, shoes that you can hike in, refillable water bottles and coffee cups, quick-dry towels and a sense of adventure.

Make room for some toys, too: snorkelling gear, fishing rods, bicycles and surfboards, kayaks or SUPs.

To reach all those secret camps and snorkelling spots that will no doubt tempt you off-road and onto sandy tracks, you'll need a reliable 4WD vehicle with recovery gear on board and some idea of how to use it. Be prepared for your phone not to work and always carry emergency supplies of water, food and fuel, plus a first aid kit, tools and basic spare car parts. It's always a good idea when heading somewhere remote and off-route to tell someone where you are headed and when you expect to be back.

REMOTE ADVENTURES

The barely populated Coral Coast is wide open and waiting for adventurers to discover, whether by 4WD, boat, kayak or on foot, but you'll need to be well prepared and self-sufficient. Carry a well-stocked first aid kit (and know how to use it) and consider packing an emergency communicator (EPIRB, inReach or similar device) to alert emergency services if something goes wrong.

Of all the weird stuff that can harm you on the Coral Coast (from blowholes and big surf to slippery walks and sharks), multi-day hikers and paddlers are most likely to suffer from dehydration. Cover up against the sun, avoid exercising in the middle of the day, drink plenty of water and wear a hat.

GETTING AROUND

From Perth to Karratha, sealed roads parallel the sea, linking almost every destination in this guidebook. But just because you stick to the bitumen doesn't mean you won't find yourself truly remote and your phone out of range. Getting to the Coral Coast's best destinations means tackling long stretches of highway, exposing you to fatigue, wandering animals and possible vehicle breakdowns.

Stick to the speed limit, give road trains plenty of room and avoid driving at night and at dawn and dusk when animals (especially kangaroos) can appear out of nowhere. If you break down or get bogged, stay with your vehicle; it will provide shelter and shade, and make you easier to locate from the air.

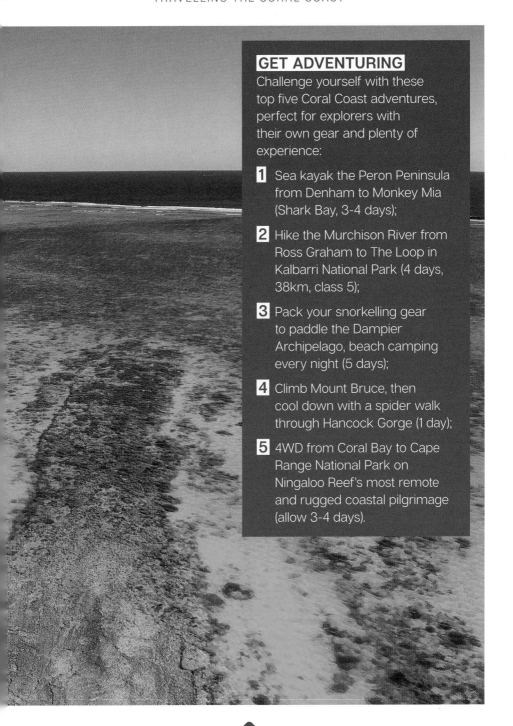

GET ADVENTURING

Challenge yourself with these top five Coral Coast adventures, perfect for explorers with their own gear and plenty of experience:

1 Sea kayak the Peron Peninsula from Denham to Monkey Mia (Shark Bay, 3-4 days);

2 Hike the Murchison River from Ross Graham to The Loop in Kalbarri National Park (4 days, 38km, class 5);

3 Pack your snorkelling gear to paddle the Dampier Archipelago, beach camping every night (5 days);

4 Climb Mount Bruce, then cool down with a spider walk through Hancock Gorge (1 day);

5 4WD from Coral Bay to Cape Range National Park on Ningaloo Reef's most remote and rugged coastal pilgrimage (allow 3-4 days).

BEACH DRIVING

All along the amazing Coral Coast, there's access to many of its beaches for well-equipped 4WDs. The ability to drive onto the sand will separate you from the crowds, helping you find remote surf locations, fishing spots and epic beach camps. But, if you haven't done much sand driving before, it can be difficult. So you make the most of your time exploring, without spending significant parts of it bogged, follow these simple tips.

LET AIR OUT OF YOUR TYRES

Not just some air, let heaps out. If you drive onto a beach with more than 20psi in the tyres, you'll probably get bogged. There is literally no more cost-effective vehicle modification you can make than to simply deflate the tyres. Deflate them until the 4WD no longer labours through the sand, but instead glides to a gentle stop when you take your foot off the accelerator, rather than lurch to one. That's usually around 15-20psi. If you get bogged, let more air out until you're not.

WATCH THE TIDES

The best time to drive on any beach is either side of low tide. That is when the beach is widest, and if you do get stuck, you've got the most time to get yourself unstuck before the tide comes back in. Only drive between the low and high tide marks to avoid damaging vegetation and dune systems, and stick to existing tracks, if there are some already.

IF YOU NEED TO TURN AROUND, TURN DOWNHILL

Driving on sand is heaps easier if you don't have to also drive up a hill. If you need to turn around while you're on the beach and go the other way, start on the high side and finish your turn on the low side, then use momentum to slowly climb back up the beach. If you start on the low side, you'll likely be at your slowest on the steepest part of the turn, and that's when you're most likely to get stuck.

STOP BEFORE YOU GET BOGGED

The key to not getting bogged is realising that you're about to be. If you can stop the car before the car is stopped, then that leaves you room to wiggle. Once you've stopped, get out and let some air out of your tyres. Then, reverse back a little until you feel your progress restricted, then drive forward a little until you feel the same. All going well, you should be able to repeat this as many times as it takes to bed a firm track of sand under the car, which you can use to gain momentum on and drive out. It might take 15 minutes, but that's easier than two hours of digging.

WEAR A SEATBELT

Just because you're off-road doesn't mean you're not responsible for your safety and that of your passengers. It's also a legal requirement to wear a seatbelt on roads and road-related areas in Australia, including beaches.

EMERGENCY+ APP

This free-to-download, Australian government-funded app can be a lifesaver. It uses the GPS functionality of your smartphone to pinpoint your exact location in the event of an emergency and mobilises emergency services to reach you as fast as possible. You just click on the app, hit 'call 000', read your GPS coordinates off the phone screen, and help will be on its way (emergencyapp.triplezero.gov.au).

NEED HELP IN AN EMERGENCY?

Phone 000 for police, ambulance or fire assistance, regardless of where you are in WA.

SAVE NINGALOO RESPECT THE REEF

How you travel on the Coral Coast directly impacts this fragile coastline, its marine ecosystems and its underwater inhabitants, many of which are endangered. Wherever you go, always abide by conservation guidelines when encountering wildlife, from nesting marine turtles and whale sharks to sea lions, emus and euro kangaroos. Never harass or chase marine mammals while swimming, be careful when fishing close to conservation and no-take zones, and never feed wildlife, no matter how much you want them to perform for your Instagram shot.

Ningaloo Reef is a rare paradise with unparalleled, easy access to travellers. As travellers, it's up to us to enjoy it without destroying it, so don't trash Ningaloo with toxic sunscreen when you swim. Surprisingly, most sunscreens sold in Australia (and elsewhere around the world) contain ingredients that have been proven to damage and bleach coral reefs. If a sunscreen contains oxybenzone (also known as benzophenone-3) and octinoxate, put it back on the shelf and find one that uses titanium dioxide to shield your skin from harmful solar rays.

INDIAN OCEAN DRIVE

From Perth's northern outskirts, the Indian Ocean Drive pulls travellers close to the sea. It hugs a wildly scenic coastline of giant shifting dunes and limestone pinnacles, dazzling blue bays where sea lions haul out, and national parks ablaze with wildflowers after winter rains.

Against these dramatic natural backdrops, sandboarders surf the largest sand crests in WA and explorers dive historical shipwrecks. Kiteboarders, anglers and paddlers find their nirvana on the sea too, while just inland, hikers wander amongst wildflowers, crunch over salt lakes and explore 300m underground through Stockyard Tunnel.

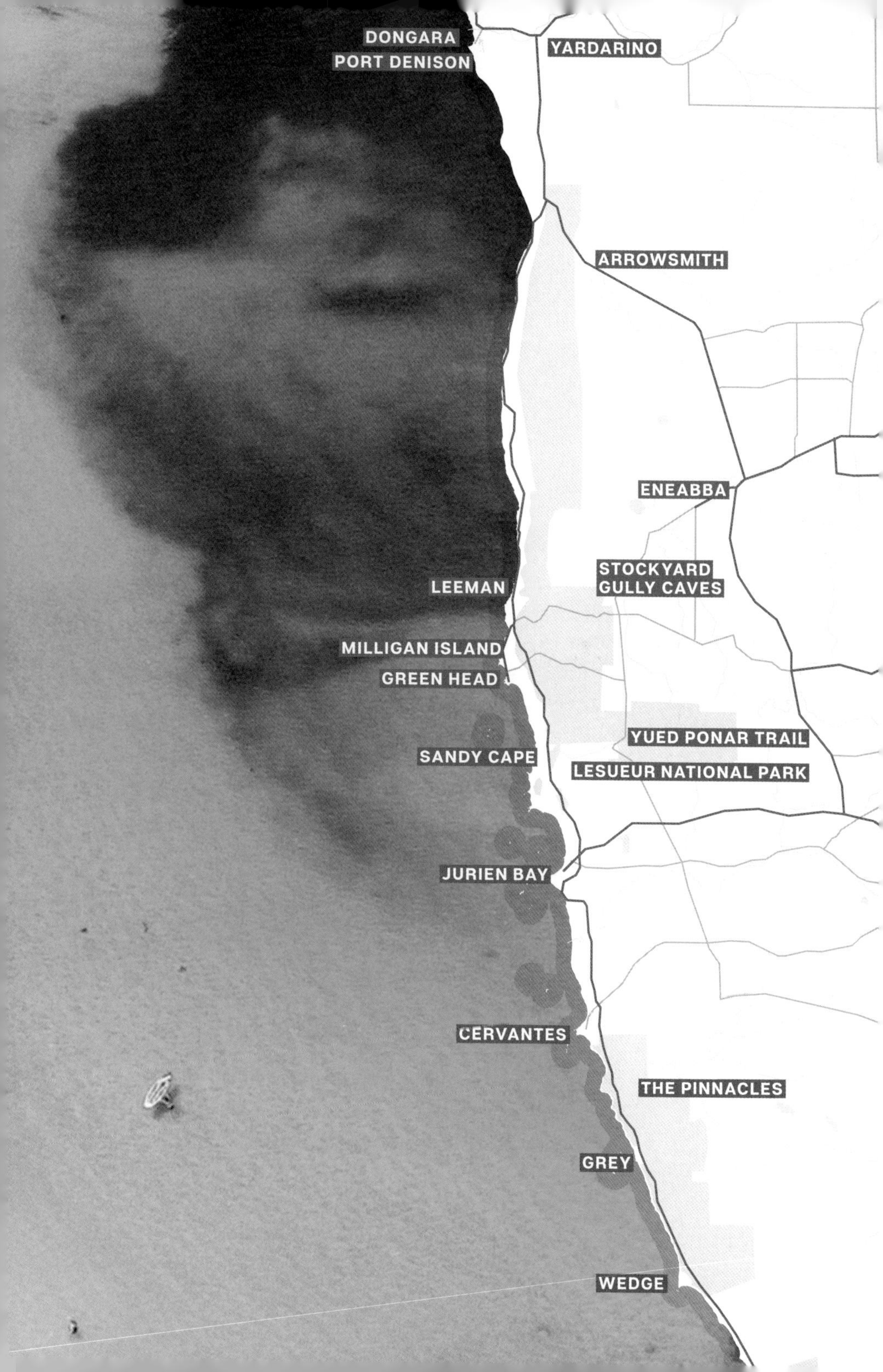
DONGARA
PORT DENISON
YARDARINO
ARROWSMITH
ENEABBA
STOCKYARD GULLY CAVES
LEEMAN
MILLIGAN ISLAND
GREEN HEAD
YUED PONAR TRAIL
SANDY CAPE
LESUEUR NATIONAL PARK
JURIEN BAY
CERVANTES
THE PINNACLES
GREY
WEDGE

You can camp atop sea cliffs, discover 3000-year-old thrombolites and swim with sea lions – all within a 270km-long drive from Yanchep to Dongara. Typical of how remote Western Australia really is, the Indian Ocean Drive didn't exist a decade ago. Now, the Turquoise Coast is accessible to all, so even though you can, you don't have to head off-road to make some memories.

If you're coming for the almost endless blue bays and white sand beaches, you can pull up right on the foreshore practically everywhere. Small fishing towns and historical beach shack settlements welcome travellers, and there are great places to eat and sleep within sight of the sea.

A beautiful Jacksonia floribunda, aka 'Holly Pea' shrub which grows up to 5m tall. Right, Leeman at sunset.

It's pretty obvious here that a connection to the ocean dominates life and livelihoods. Generations-old lobster fleets work Australia's largest single-species fishery, while inland, the sublime Mediterranean climate nurtures olives, wine grapes, citrus and beautiful, blooming wildflowers.

Historically there's a lot to explore, and not surprisingly, much of what fascinates history buffs (and divers, boaties and snorkellers) lies under the sea. European explorers, many of whom first set their sights on Australia here in the 1600s, sailed dangerously close to the coast, littering the seabed with their shipwrecks and giving rise to harrowing tales of seamanship and survival. Theirs are the stories that transform this tranquil coastline into something more sobering, so jump at the chance to get yourself offshore and exploring, either aboard a tour boat or by bringing your own tinny or kayak.

Before European discoveries, however, this region belonged to the Yued group of the Noongar peoples. They tell of Wagyl, the rainbow serpent, who weaved throughout the land carving out rivers and landmarks like the world-famous Pinnacles and opalescent Dynamite Bay at Green Head. These are the places you'll connect with too as you travel north, so take your time. Even if the kilometres seem easy to conquer, all that you'll discover here deserves an unhurried pace.

LANCELIN $^1/_{100}$ ☐
SAND AND SURF

01

A dose of adrenaline in the sandhills north of Perth.

Lancelin's towering sand dunes are the biggest in the west, luring speed demons of all ages to shred the sand on boards, bikes and 4WD vehicles too. Perched on the edge of two kilometres of pure white sand waves, thrill-seekers ride sandboards (and boogie boards), quad and trail bikes, dazzling onlookers with their daring descents and some seriously sandy spills.

Mid-morning, when the winds are lightest, is the best time to get sand

surfing, and you can rent a proper sandboard in town (from just $12.50) or BYO boogie boards. The dunes are kid-friendly and easy to find: head north through town onto Beacon Street, turn right onto Desert Drive and follow the compacted right-hand track to the bottom of the dunes. 2WD vehicles can park and walk in, but off-roading gets you deeper to more secluded slopes.

When Lancelin's gusty afternoon sea breezes kick in, it's time to head for the sea, to surf, kiteboard and windsurf the shallow bays that make this one of the best boarding destinations in the country. South of town, Back Beach gathers surfers from March to June with tempered south-westerly swells (mornings are best), while kiteboarders favour the summer months for the strong south-easterly winds that also lure marathon windsurfers to join Lancelin's world-famous Ocean Classic.

If you're not chasing thrills, Lancelin's impossibly blue bay will keep you busy with islands to visit and incredible daily catches (it's Indigenous name Wangaree means 'fish' after all!). An extensive offshore reef system, that has wrecked fourteen ships and created a world-famous dive trail, nurtures Western rock lobsters and dhufish, pink snapper, yellowtail kingfish and baldchin groper too. You can launch your boat off the sand near the jetty, and throw a line here to snare tailor, flathead and whiting at dusk and dawn.

Just 700m offshore, Lancelin Island provides sanctuary to seabirds and the odd sea lion too, with a boardwalk and access for private boats along its western and eastern shores. If you love to SUP or kayak, close-to-shore Edward Island is easy to reach on calm days, and grommets will love the local skate park's half-pipe and cool pump track. Find out more at **lancelin.com.au**.

01 Sandboarding is a popular pastime in Lancelin, especially when there's no surf.

02 The dunes are constantly shifting, so every visit offers something new.

03 Bring a 4WD to explore further.

01

Sun, surf and a controversial slice of WA holiday history.

Sporting "Save Wedge" bumper stickers on 4WDs piled high with camping gear, Perth's beach-loving city escapees spend their rustic weekends at Wedge, staking out historical shacks and filling long sandy days at the water's edge. They fish, surf and embrace a slice of the simple life that dates back to the 1940s, long before Wedge Island Point and Grey (15km north), became Australia's largest and most controversial shack settlements.

Pioneered in 1937 by weekend fishermen W.R. (Bob) Wedge and his friends, a wave of like-minded followers soon erected tents, built timber-and-tin huts, and established tight-knit communities that have since flourished in the hands of grandchildren and great-grandchildren who cherished their simple summertime escapes.

Today, controversy surrounds the off-the-grid dwellings that hold a shaky tenure to this coastline. Since 1989, the WA government has fought to demolish the settlements against the overwhelming will of the people

who treasure the shacks' historical significance and the protection they afford the local ecology against mainstream tourism development.

Visitors will find both Wedge and Grey equally fascinating, not only for the old shack architecture and the self-sufficient residents you are likely to meet, but because all of it preserves a coastal lifestyle that's all but disappeared elsewhere in Australia.

Both Wedge and Grey are open communities and welcome visitors to explore the white sand beaches and bright blue bays that drew residents to their shacks long ago. On the low tide at Wedge, you can walk across the exposed bar to explore the island, and at Grey, you can paddle or boat across the windy bay to discover Green, Whittell and Buller Islands.

01 The tin shacks of Wedge and Grey date back to the 1930s and 40s, with sprawling additions over the years.

02 Wedge Island is a popular surfing destination, away from the crowds.

THE PINNACLES 3/100 □

Size yourself up against these crumbling limestone spires.

Casting shadows across the ancient Spearwood dunes, the Pinnacle's weathered limestone pillars stud a golden vista, rising up to four metres high in all kinds of strangely phallic guises. They steal the show in Nambung National Park, where you can take a scenic drive through the desert dunes, and head out on foot, climbing the shifting sands to capture more and more enigmatic scenes.

The ever-popular Pinnacles are one of the west's biggest tourism drawcards, so to find yourself alone, set out along the gentle Emu Walk Trail at dusk or dawn. When the crowds thin out, western grey kangaroos emerge from beneath the acacias to graze and vamp up your photos too. Most of the park's animals are nocturnal but, proving there is life in the desert, more than 90 bird species call the park home.

Covering a tremendous area of the Swan Coastal Plain, the Pinnacles baffled early Dutch explorers who, it's said, mistook the limestone spires for the ancient ruins of a long-abandoned city. Constantly buried and revealed again by the shifting, marching sand dunes, the

Pinnacles have long been woven into Indigenous Yued folklore, representing a symbol of peace in the land.

In the quiet, golden hours that bookend the tourist crush at the Pinnacles, you'll find solitude and peace. Arrive early for cool weather exploring, then escape the heat indoors and get the grand geology lesson at the Pinnacles Desert Discovery Centre (open 9:30 am to 4:30 pm). If you have the time, return at dusk to capture the Pinnacles in the glowing, sunset light.

Located 245km north of Perth, Nambung National Park provides no campgrounds, so overnight, instead,

01 Sunset is the best time to visit.

02 Walking or driving the Pinnacles is the best way to explore the limestone pillars.

in nearby Cervantes or at Nambung Station Stay. Beyond the Pinnacles there's plenty to do: swim with surfing dolphins at stunning Hangover Bay, cook up a barbecue beside the Aussie animals that gave Kangaroo Point its name, and take a walk beside baffling living fossils at Lake Thetis. National park entry costs $15 per vehicle, and the best time to visit is from September to October when the park bristles with wildflowers (**parks.dpaw.wa.gov.au**).

LAKE THETIS $^4/_{100}$ ☐

01

Discover 3000-year-old living fossils, responsible for our every breath!

Thriving in a hypersaline lake that's twice as salty as the sea, the stromatolites and thrombolites that girth Lake Thetis are living examples of the earth's very first organisms. Grey and unimpressive they may be, but what these ancient lumps of cyanobacteria can do with an excess of saltwater and sunshine is exciting stuff.

They are singlehandedly credited with creating all life on earth (well, at least the oxygen that gave life to everything on the planet, allowing complex life forms to evolve and eventually, humans too).

Rare stromatolites are found in only two well-developed areas on the planet (Shark Bay and the Bahamas) and exist in small numbers at Lake Thetis along with more common thrombolites. To see them up close, a 1.5km-long walking trail loops around the lake (the best examples are found just 300 metres along the boardwalk).

Named for the sailing ship 'Thetis' that surveyed the coast from 1847 to 1848, Lake Thetis lies within the protective boundary of Nambung National Park, close to the Pinnacles. Winter is the best time to visit when the lake's water level is low, making the stromatolites and thrombolites more visible. To get there, follow the signs 1.7km south-east of Cervantes.

STAY

This whole stretch of coast really suits travellers who are either flexible or self-sufficient.

Camping options abound, and there's everything from obscure free camps down bumpy red-dirt roads to flashy popular family resorts. There are not a lot of options for 'five-star' luxury, but if you turn to share sites like Airbnb, there's no shortage of beachside apartments and houses that are pretty flash.

MILLIGAN ISLAND CAMPING NODE

NAMBUNG STATION STAY

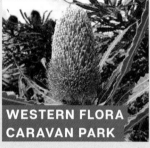

WESTERN FLORA CARAVAN PARK

Of all the beachfront camps along the Indian Ocean Drive, Milligan Island, north of Green Head, is one of the best. Catering strictly to campers, 36 spacious sites have uninterrupted ocean views. There are shade shelters, barbecues and toilets, dogs on leads are welcome, and you can stay for up to three nights. Fees are $15 per night (per vehicle), collected by a ranger (bring cash; there's an ATM in the Green Head General Store). You'll need to bring drinking water too.

This family favourite working sheep and cattle station occupies 5,000 acres of countryside. Out here the air is fresh, wildlife is abundant and the Milky Way is the star attraction every evening. Unpowered sites begin at $30 a night or $40 with power, per couple. There are on-site caravans for $80 per night or a two bedroom bed and breakfast with a shared kitchen and bathroom for $140 per night including continental breakfast. The farm tour is highly recommended $20 per person, $10 for kids. **nambungstation.com.au**

So much more than a caravan park, this accommodation hub with cabins, mud-brick chalets and campsites is also a haven for wildlife, located on 160 acres in prime wildflower country. There are daily guided wildflower walks from August to October at 4:30 pm, 12km of walking tracks to explore for wild encounters with birds, kangaroos, blue-tongued lizards and ten species of frog. Pets are welcome (on a leash), fuel is available, and there are plenty of accommodation options. **westernfloracp. com**

JURIEN BAY'S $^5/_{100}$ □
AUSSIE SEA LIONS

01

Go wild swimming with one of the world's rarest sea lions.

Curious, playful and distinctly Australian, the sea lions of Jurien Bay dazzle snorkellers, somersaulting and twirling through the turquoise sea. Encounters with one of the world's rarest sea lion species have put Jurien Bay firmly on the map, luring snorkellers onto tour boats bound for rocky offshore isles.

Found along Australia's southern shores from Kangaroo Island to WA's Houtman-Abrolhos Islands, Australian sea lions are considered endangered or threatened at best. Their wild population of around 10,000 to 12,000 is in serious decline. They are unusually slow to reproduce (gestation takes a whopping 17 months), and life spans in the wild may be as short as eight to nine years.

Jurien Bay's 800-strong breeding colony hauls out on three isolated isles – Buller Island, North Fisherman Island and Essex Rocks – all safeguarded by a marine sanctuary that prioritises the sea lions instead of the fishing activities that threaten their survival.

Access to all three spots is restricted so you'll need to join a tour, and itineraries often include a dive over the underwater pinnacles, whale watching and dolphin spotting too. This coastline is deemed a temperate version of WA's Ningaloo Reef, and extensive seagrass meadows nurture western rock lobsters, and a huge variety of sea life thrives. If you've packed a wetsuit, there are shallow dive and snorkelling sites off Boullanger Island in up to six metres of water.

Close to the coast, you'll find coral bommies right off Jurien Bay's Town Beach, and an underwater snorkelling trail begins at the old Jetty, exploring a colourful artificial reef nurtured in six metres of water, complete with interpretive signs buried into the seafloor. Local shops sell underwater swim cards for a small donation to help you identify the fish species you are likely to encounter.

Jurien Bay has accommodation for budgets, but if you love to beach camp surrounded by sweeping white dunes, head for Sandy Cape Recreation Area, 13km north of town. The facilities are considered excellent, pets are permitted, and the angling keeps campers smiling (**visitturquoisecoast. com.au**).

01 In Jurien Bay, you can swim with the puppy dogs of the sea by joining a snorkelling tour.

02 Is it still a selfie if someone else takes it for you?

03 There's something so romantic about sunsets over the sea.

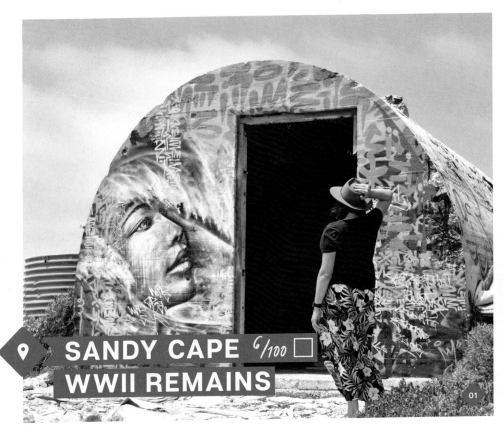

SANDY CAPE ⁶/₁₀₀ ☐
WWII REMAINS

Secluded beaches, 4WD exploring and rare WWII ruins.

When the possibility of a Japanese invasion threatened WA during World War II, 22 military radar stations were set up along the sparsely populated coastline. Few of these historical posts remain today, making Radar Station 48 at North Head, 10km north of Jurien Bay, something of a state treasure.

The site dates back to 1943, and although most of the original buildings have long since been removed, two generator igloos, concrete sandbag reinforcements and an underground tank remain on site. An archaeological survey in 2016 unearthed a host of relics from the surrounding dunes, including 303 casings and bullet projectiles, glass bottles, bully beef tins, an iron tent peg and bones.

The site's popularity as a fishing camp means that graffiti now adorns what's left, but it's hoped that heritage protection will be afforded to Radar Station 48 in the near future. When you visit, discover and enjoy, but leave all relics on-site to preserve their historical context and this rare military ruins.

Here's the part where we tell you how to get there. Access is 4WD-only and heads south from the campground at Sandy Cape Recreation Area following the rocky coastal track. Go past the blowholes and onto a sand track (lower your tyre pressure to around 15 to 20psi), park your car and walk the final 150 metres to the ruins.

Sandy Cape is a hugely popular camping destination on this stretch of coast, where $20 buys you one of 88 breezy beach campsites just a few steps from the sand. There are sea lions to spot and so many curling bays to paddle, snorkel and swim, and you can 4WD along the beach to reach secluded, faraway fishing spots and more remote beach campsites away from the fray. Don't forget a board to surf the towering sand dunes behind camp.

Facilities at Sandy Cape just seem to keep improving: toilets, barbecue and picnic areas, a dump point and non-potable water tanks. Access is 2WD and pets on leads are welcome, but no bookings are taken so you'll need to arrive early to beat the crowds over the busy winter travel season. Bring drinking water, plenty of beach toys and cash to pay for camping fees ($20/night for two adults and up to two kids). To get there, turn off the Indian Ocean Drive 10km north of Jurien Bay and continue 7km to camp.

01 These two, 5m long concrete 'igloos' are military ruins, dating back to 1943.

02 Each igloo housed a generator that ran the Radar Station 48 during WWII.

03 4WD along the beach to discover some great fishing and sandboarding spots.

Walk through wildflowers on one of WA's newest short hikes.

Nurturing a staggering rollcall of wildflowers, Lesueur National Park is one of WA's most important reserves. A whopping 10 per cent of all west coast plants are found here.

Created in 2019 to reveal the best of Lesueur National Park over eight spectacular kilometres, the Yued Ponar Trail (class 4, 3-4hrs return) sets out through colourful lowland heath and wildflower meadows before the trail climbs steadily up the edge of the plateau to the summit of Mount Peron for startling ocean views. Inland, the flat-top mesa of Mount Lesueur stands guard, and views from Kada Boodja lookout provide spectacular vistas.

Along the way, interpretive signs reveal the six seasons recognised by the Yued Noongar peoples who favour djilba (August and September) or kambarang (October and November) as the best seasons for wildflowers.

For a shorter way to explore, you could tackle the easy Botanical Path (400m), the Gairdner Walk Trail (2.5km, class 3), or the Lesueur Walk Trail (4km, class 3). Back on the bitumen, the Lesueur Scenic Drive leads past Mount Lesueur to Cockleshell Gully where ubiquitous grasstrees grow (18.5km). Wildflower seekers can tick off 11 species endemic to this region, including the honey bush (hakea), magenta starflower, Lesueur hakea, cork mallee and the unusual propeller banksia.

Park entry costs $15 per vehicle ($8 for concession cardholders), but for longer stays in WA, a Holiday Parks Pass (4 weeks, $60) or an Annual Parks Pass (1 year, $120) make sound investments.

EAT

If you love fresh seafood, you'll love the casual, easy dining along the Indian Ocean Drive.

It's not hard to find great fish and chips or super fresh seafood everywhere along this stretch of coast. You could probably even barter for it at campsites. For something a little different, these three eateries are our faves.

ILLEGAL TENDER RUM CO.

STARFISH CAFE

LOBSTER SHACK

This is more of a liquid meal, but we won't judge. The small-batch rum distillery ages its spirits for two years in oak barrels, named after the unofficial currency banned under William Bligh. You can enjoy it at the cellar door or in the onsite restaurant, The Common Place. If you're coming from Dongara or Port Denison via Springfield Drive, turn east onto Ironbark Road, left onto Sheoak, then right down Illyarrie, rather than trusting Google. 35 Illyarrie Rd, Springfield. **illegaltenderrumco.com**

The go-to cafe in Port Denison with an old-school, beach shack vibe, bean bags, corrugated iron walls and views over the beach. It serves up some seriously good coffee and a menu of healthy, hearty, meals too. They also stock a range of gorgeous ceramic cups with designs inspired by striking west coast landscapes. This is the place to come if you just need a casual, satisfying meal in a great location. South Beach, Port Denison. **facebook.com/ starfishsouthbeach**

The Shack is a bit of a local institution and much more than a great place to feast. WA's lobster industry is one of the largest single-species fisheries in Australia, and the Lobster Shack is as close to a 'farm gate' as you'll get. Here you can take a self-guided tour to see how rock lobsters are processed once they reach the shore, and afterwards, sit down to sample some, feasting on all kinds of seafood at a restaurant overlooking the sea. 37 Catalonia Street, Cervantes. **lobstershack.com.au**

DYNAMITE BAY 8/100 ☐

A heavenly beach haven with a treasure-hunting history.

Bound by rugged cliffs and a crescent of white silica sand, this near-perfect turquoise cove should be far more popular than it is. Until the secret gets out, you can SUP, snorkel and swim in calm waters protected by great fingers of rock.

Tracks lead up to either side of the bay where you can take in the unforgettable ocean vistas and catch a sunrise. Within easy reach, Dynamite Bay Takeaway knows how to use an espresso machine, and can sate hungry appetites after long stints in the sea.

The origin of the name Dynamite Bay is shrouded in local folklore. Some say its name comes from a band of 1960s treasure hunters who used a Dutch map to locate the shipwreck of the

Vergulde Draeck. The treasure hunters supposedly used dynamite to excavate the ship's bounty of silver coins from the seabed. Others say the bay was named for the fisherman that once used sticks of dynamite to stun fish.

There's plenty more to explore north of Green Head. Here, Anchorage Bay stretches endlessly past a jetty and boat ramp to a top surf break at distant Point Louise where you can snorkel inside the reef too. Three Bays Walkway provides Green Head's grand coastal tour, luring hikers from South Bay to Dynamite Bay and onto Anchorage Bay too (2.5km).

With just a few places to stay, Green Head lacks the hustle and bustle of fishing hubs found elsewhere on the coast, which is exactly what you want if surfing and snorkelling are on your to-do list. Visit in early autumn for cool weather and warm sea temperatures.

LEEMAN ⁹/₁₀₀ ☐

The most laid-back coastal fishing haven on the coast.

Taking its name from the town's most successful castaway, Leeman has a long, salty heritage. Rock lobster fishing fuels local livelihoods, and visitors cherish unhurried holidays, arriving with fishing gear and boats in tow.

Leeman is named after Abraham Leeman van Santwits. Leeman had survived not only the sinking of the Vergulde Draeck back in 1656, but a subsequent month-long voyage back to Batavia (now Jakarta, Indonesia) in a small, open boat. Incredibly, when Leeman returned two years later as navigator aboard the Waeckende Boey, history repeated when he and some

crew were marooned on Fisherman Island with a damaged small boat and only meagre supplies. Leeman embarked on a second, treacherous attempt to journey back to Java and, heroically, survived.

Today, serving up salty, sand-on-your-feet holidays is what Leeman does best. With protected boat ramps, surf breaks, and enough catches of dhufish to please the boaties, this town has the slow life down pat. If you can't land a catch, the Leeman Fish And Chip Shop, on Spencer Street, comes to the rescue with fresh, local seafood with that laid back, beach-shell-and-driftwood vibe that's so typically WA. Its alfresco dining area is the perfect place to relax on a warm, summer arvo too.

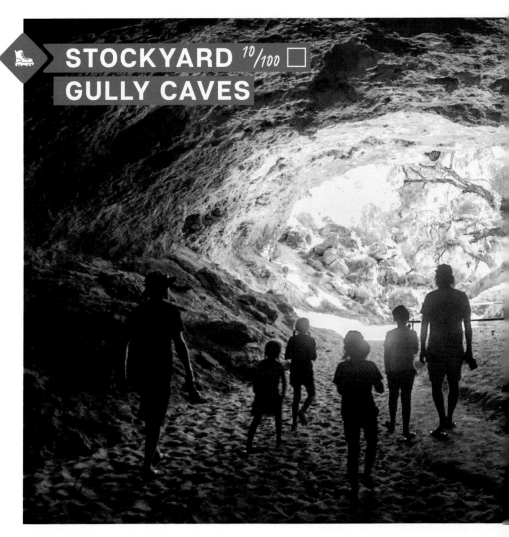

STOCKYARD GULLY CAVES

Spotlight your way through an inky, underground tunnel.

Providing one of the best beginner caving experiences in the west, Stockyard Tunnel disappears for 300 metres, luring self-guided walkers along an ancient limestone seabed through the inky darkness. It's a thrilling place to explore with tiny stalactites and solution pipes dripping overhead, and along the cave walls, deep crevices and tight squeezes to climb and peer into.

Stockyard Tunnel occasionally floods so it lacks the extensive, glittering formations you might find elsewhere. Instead, its rock walls are coloured in

01

colourful gully shaded by flooded gums and stunning zamia palms. Enormous feral beehives and the mud nests of welcome swallows cling to the high limestone walls, and after winter rains, vibrant wildflowers burst into bloom.

Around 150 years ago, this was a popular drovers' rest, favoured for the shade and water it offered and the natural 'stockyard' that the tunnel and gullies at either end provided. Today, Stockyard Gully National Park provides an easy, hour-long loop that takes you through the tunnel and returns along a sunnier trail, winding past wild wintertime blooms of orange Christmas trees, Queen of Sheba orchids, yellow leschenaultia, and the ubiquitous banksias that feed honeyeaters and elusive honey possums.

This hidden oasis is an ideal place to escape the midday heat and charges no entry fees. There are picnic facilities (bring drinking water) and toilets, but be warned: access is strictly four-wheel drive. From the Indian Ocean Drive between Leeman and Green Head, turn east onto Coorow-Green Head Road, drive for 14.5km, then turn north onto unsealed Cockleshell Gully Road and continue for 15km. If you need to fill your tanks, Leeman has a reputation for selling the cheapest fuel on the Coral Coast.

subtle hues of pink and yellow from iron oxides, haematite and goethite, and delicate decorations form only where floodwaters can't reach.

It takes about 15 minutes to explore the cave, flicking off your torch midway to discover what pitch-black really means. Before long, a welcoming glow lures you out the other side into a lush,

01 Bring a torch for each of the kids and ignite their sense of discovery as they enjoy their very own Indiana Jones adventure.

01

Drive, walk and explore the wonders in Kwongan country.

The Noongar people call this country Kwongan: a great sandy plain that once covered a third of south-west Australia, bristling with vibrant, hardy wildflowers all winter long. Although much reduced by land clearing today, great swathes of Kwongan survives, springing from soil so dry and lacking in nutrients, you'll marvel at how such dazzling Aussie wildflowers bloom at all.

When they do, they lure droves of onlookers on a wild, flowery adventure to the Eneabba (pronounced En-ee-ab-a) Sandplain, 27km from the coast. Turn inland off the Indian Ocean Drive, where Beekeepers Nature Reserve flanks the road, to Lake Indoon (for free camping), and continue to Tathra National Park, 28km east of Eneabba.

The Noongar people got it right when they named Tathra – the 'beautiful place' – for here you'll marvel at stunning kangaroo paws, orange banksias and the endemic daviesia (bitter peas), and spot emus, echidnas, kangaroos and even a pair of breeding eagles too.

02

When it fills after winter rains, Lake Indoon transforms into a drought refuge for wildlife and a staging post for long-haul birds on their north-south migratory route. A full lake attracts waterskiers and paddlers too, who set up camp in the shade of rare, towering flooded gums. Camping is free for up to three nights, pets are welcome, and there's a boat ramp, coldwater showers, toilets, and a picnic shelter with free gas barbecues. You'll find it signposted 18km off the Indian Ocean Road along the Coolimba-Eneabba Road. Check with council if the lake is open before heading there.

01 The ephemeral Lake Indoon, filled with winter rain.

02 The rare Rose of the West, known to Noongar people as mottlecah.

Kwongan country nurtures a whopping 8600 flora and fauna species, and you can see a fair chunk in the reserves surrounding Eneabba. When it flowers in April, look for the rare Rose of the West, a small mallee shrub with huge pinky-red flowers that Noongar people call mottlecah. Its bold red-to-pink flowers, yellow anthers and silver coloured leaves make for a striking contrast on an already unusual looking plant. It also has beautiful, silvery gum nuts.

DONGARA 12/100 □
DENISON DRIVE-IN

01

An old school drive-in for starry night flicks.

It might be home to a million-dollar fishing fleet, but Dongara-Port Denison's best night out is down-to-earth and decidedly old school. Just about every Saturday night for more than 50 years, the twin towns' rare, starry night cinema has been gathering and entertaining movie-goers under the stars. The food is cheap, dogs are welcome, and movie screenings raise money for Dongara-Port Denison's community groups and clubs too.

This is a night out that really winds back the clock and, with only two drive-in cinemas still operating in Western Australia (the other is in Kununurra), you won't want to miss this starry night movie screening. The cinema is located on Point Leander Drive at Port Denison. Gates open at 5 pm and movies kick-off when darkness falls, usually after 7 pm. For movie details, check out the Dongara Denison Drive-In Facebook page.

Dongara-Port Denison rates as one of the most traveller-friendly hubs around, offering free Wi-Fi and free waterfront campgrounds too. You can spend up to three nights free camping on the south coast at Cliff Head, Fresh Water Point and Knobby Head. Back in town, there's free Wi-Fi at the information centre and along the Port Denison waterfront where you can grab a coffee from the Green Beanie coffee cart at Granny Beach, scroll your daily feed and enjoy some breezy sea views.

SURF

For a stretch of road that hugs the coast so tightly, it's never really far from good surfing opportunities. If you crave regular immersion in salty water, fibreglass in hand, you'll want to bookmark these spots.

Although it's WA's far south and mid-north that are best known for world-class surf spots, this short stretch between Lancelin and Cervantes has its own humble array of decent waves. Although much of the coast is protected by off-shore reef systems, the swell does break through in places, and if you're prepared for an early morning session, you'll get fun waves.

BACK BEACH, LANCELIN

WEDGE ISLAND

POINT LOUISE, GREEN HEAD

Back Beach gathers surfers from March to June with tempered south-westerly swells (mornings are best), while kiteboarders favour the summer months for the strong south-easters that also lure marathon windsurfers. If you have a 4WD, drive right onto the beach via a track at the main carpark and search for the best bank. If you have a boat, explore the offshore reef to the north.

Most surfers from Jurien Bay head to Wedge Island when there's swell on tap (it's best from the west or south west). South of the island, the beach stretches for kilometres, offering multiple beach breaks and a few rocky reefs. Best of all, you can explore its length in a 4WD and set up in front of the best looking peak. It's a great place to learn if you're new to surfing, with often long, small waves.

This picturesque point north of Green Head is one of the best-known waves in the region, breaking both right and left off the reef just off the lookout. It's pretty shallow on low tide and often needs a decent swell running for it to be worth the hassle, but when it's good, it's lots of fun and hard enough to get to that crowds are rare. No swell? You can snorkel amongst the reef inside.

GERALDTON AND WILDFLOWER COUNTRY

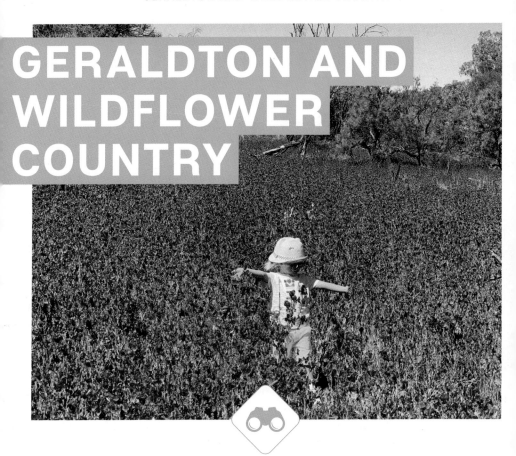

Colour dominates Geraldton and its surrounding land and seascapes. Every year after winter rains, the coast's farms and fields bristle with grandiose displays of more than 12,000 wildflower species.

Where land meets sea, pristine white beaches pair with turquoise waters, often painted by a rainbow of sails and kites as windsurfers pursue their passion in the afternoon sea breezes. Even the landmarks are colourful, like the candy-cane striped lighthouse that stands guard over the coast.

When the sea calms, you could spend your time flitting from one spectacular white-sand beach to the next or wandering inland over never-ending fields of wildflowers. Each time you visit this ever-changing region, there'll be a new favourite cafe, boutique or unique museum exhibition to wander through. During summer, when the afternoon sea breeze kicks in from the south, warm water and big waves bring out the kiteboarders and windsurfers to work their magic and woo onlookers.

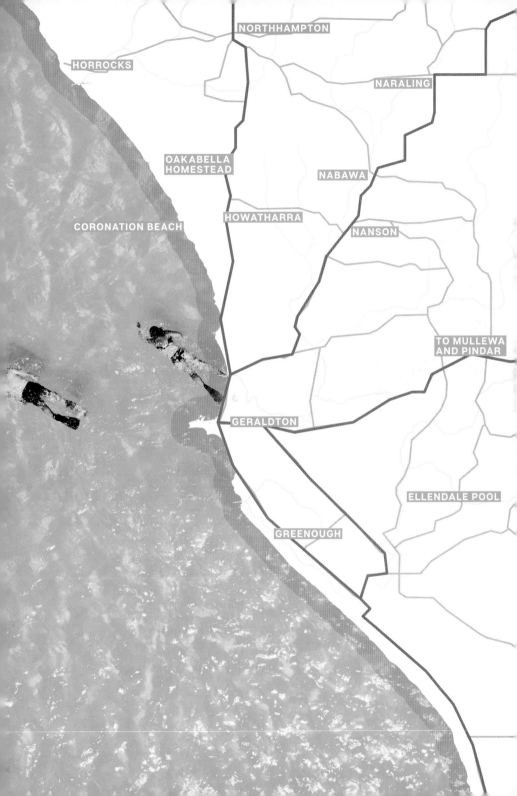

Action and adventure aside, there's a whole lot of history to unearth too. For tens of thousands of years, the Amangu, Nanda and Watjarri peoples have called this region home, and their vivid stories resonate as you paddle Ellendale Pool or stroll through the Ilgarijiri (Things Belonging To The Sky) Sculptures on the Esplanade. The region's European historical past is no less diverse.

Shipwrecks pepper Geraldton's coastline, each with epic and tragic tales that you can unearth at the town's world-class museum. Stroll through 100-year-old cathedrals as exquisite as any you'd find in Rome, or revel in world history and culture through a quirky collection of biscuit tins.

A lone Western Australian Christmas tree, heralding times of warmer weather.

Geraldton is the self-proclaimed lobster capital of the world. It's home to the largest single-species fishery in Australia, and fishers here haul out 6500 tonnes of western rock lobster each year. Fishing has dominated its culture and employment opportunities for decades, making it the best place on this coastline to get fresh seafood (unless you catch it yourself).

But ultimately, it's wildflowers that steal the show. They bloom en masse from late July to October, and incredibly, new species are being discovered every season. And although they might look pretty, these hardy little blooms have some remarkable survival skills. Some trap and feed off insects, others bloom only at night, and others – like the wreath flower – baffle us with their unique, circular formations.

Far away from any big-city lights, this region is an astrophotographer's dream, and the Milky Way beams brighter than you've ever seen on clear wintery nights. Warm, sunny days and consistent summertime winds lure thousands of travellers to camp by the beach or relax in seaside rentals in Geraldton's picturesque coastal hamlets.

Whatever you come to indulge in, you'll enjoy fresh air, starry nights, turquoise ocean dips and fields of colour that stretch to the far horizon. This stunning part of West Oz should attract far bigger crowds than it does. Thankfully, it's all waiting, just for you.

STAY

Whether you're scouring the coast for water-based adventure or hiking inland to experience wildflowers at their best, you'll sleep easy each night.

From beachfront, national park campsites to fully-featured family resorts and quaint B&Bs, this stretch of coast suits people on the move or those looking to settle in. Here are some great places to stay.

BELAIR GARDENS CARAVAN PARK

Like so many 'caravan parks' these days, Belair is an all-encompassing family resort on the best real-estate in Geraldton. Right out on the edge of Point Moore, in the shadow of the lighthouse, the park has excellent cabins, holiday units and powered campsites. Walking distance to everything on the foreshore, camp from $30 or book a cabin from $90, depending on the season. The park is pet friendly, has a playground, camp kitchen and a pool. summerstar.com.au

OLD PINDAR HOTEL

Although the federation-style pub was centrepiece of Pindar during its heyday as a thriving railway town, Pindar declined and the hotel closed late in the 1970s. In 2019 it was bought by a young family, who have been slowly restoring it while offering a charming bed and breakfast. It's a real step back into good ol' fashioned hospitality. Accomodation options include glamping tents and sumptuous cheese platters and fireside meals. facebook.com/oldpindarhotel

LITTLE BAY CAMPSITE

Just five minutes north of Horrocks, Little Bay is one of the best campsites on the whole coast. With 4WD access only, campers are lucky enough to park up at the sandy beach for only $15 a carload! More sheltered than most places from the howling winds of the west, Little Bay has a beautiful lagoon, sand dunes that light up magnificently as the sun sets, and the cherry on top is that you're allowed to have a campfire. The only facilities are long-drop toilets.

Unrivalled stargazing in the heart of wheat country.

It's been a centrepiece of community life since this tiny Wheatbelt town first began; one of the first buildings erected and something of a survivor too. When Cyclone Hazel razed the

hall back in 1979, local townspeople called for a referendum and fought for its restoration. Today, Yandanooka Hall studs a near-deserted main street, but astrophotographers and travellers gather here to stargaze every night at dusk.

The town, whose Indigenous name means 'water in the hills', has a proud pastoral

01

All of Mingenew Shire lies within Australia's designated radio quiet zone, so there's little interference from radio communications, and almost no light pollution. This creates perfect conditions to observe the cosmos, and on any given night, you can join avid stargazers gazing skyward. Bring your telescope or make friends with someone who's brought one. There are toilets and camping is allowed for up to three days.

When you visit the shire, look out for the show-stopping emu tree or bottlebrush hakea (hakea francisiana) that flowers between July and October. These striking trees grow to heights of eight metres and bloom with vibrant pink flowers equally adored by honeyeaters and bouquets. In summer, Nuytsia floribunda, or WA Christmas tree dot the roadsides and fields. Christmas trees have long been known to the Noongar people as moodjar, who say the trees hold the spirits of their ancestors. It blooms consistently October to December, signalling the arrival of Christmas, and is believed to be the largest parasitic tree in the world. It takes moisture and nutrients from almost anything green within a 110-metre radius, including grasses, weeds, shrubs and eucalypts.

heritage that dates back to the late 1800s when big-name WA pastoralists the Emanuels and Forrests came to town. Yandanooka's heyday came with the settlement of returned WWII servicemen, but the dust has settled over this sleepy spot, making it one of the best places in the region for stargazing.

01 Yandanooka Hall welcomes travellers to park up for 72 hours and enjoy the night skies that the region is famous for.

GREENOUGH $^{14}/_{100}$ ☐
CENTRAL HISTORIC AREA

01

Discover WA's famous leaning trees and an entire historical village preserved in stone.

On rolling hills sculpted by an unrelenting wind, Greenough's stunning, stunted trees bow close to the earth in great supplicating groves. Indigenous poet Nola Gregory described it best in 'The Leaning Trees'...."I am Wirnda Ngadara, the leaning tree, I have grown this way, from too much breeze, my twisted trunk, bowed down to search, and pay respect, to my Mother Earth".

It's the combination of super-salty air and great southerly winds that fold Greenough's red river gums (eucalyptus camaldulensis) to face north, creating a spectacle that literally stops traffic on the Brand Highway. Grab your photos from the dedicated rest stop on the southern side of Central Greenough, then drive north to wander through this mid-nineteenth century village, gloriously restored and maintained by the National Trust.

From a prosperous wheat-growing town to a ghost town in just 90 years,

Greenough endured droughts, cyclones and floods, a gold rush and wheat rust before World War II dealt the final blow and deserted the town. Today, significant restoration projects have brought Greenough back to life, offering visitors a rare wander back in time through 11 distinguished stone buildings, including the open-air museum, the miller's residence, a school, police station, Catholic church, Anglican church and Maleys Bridge.

Built in the town's old store, the Central Greenough Cafe serves up good coffee, meals and irresistible baked treats and now serves as the cellar door for Copperhead Road Distillery, which tempts with free tastings and sales of locally made rum, liqueurs and absinthe. The adjacent museum and visitor centre is open daily from 9 am to 3 pm. Entry is free for National Trust Members, $10 for adults and $5 for kids (five years or less are free), and you can pat and feed the resident llamas and alpacas for free. Find it 22km south of Geraldton on the Brand Highway. centralgreenough.com

A great little detour (that few travellers find) takes you 10km north to the Greenough River Mouth at Cape Burney, where you can park your car and walk, or 4WD south across the river to some little limestone beach caves just perfect for sunset picnics. The river mouth rarely opens to the ocean, so the crossing is usually quite easy; just pack beach toys and plenty of supplies.

01 St Peter's Catholic Church was built in 1908.

02 Wesleyan Methodist Chapel was built in 1867.

03 Strong coastal winds and salty air have an amazing affect on the local trees.

ELLENDALE $^{15}/_{100}$ ☐
POOL

01

Waterhole camping in a 'mini Kimberley' gorge.

Beneath towering cliffs scoured out by the Greenough River, campers set up along the deep, welcoming waterhole at Ellendale, striking campfires and launching kayaks and SUPs to explore. Giant gum trees throw shade, the facilities are a cut above the rest, and at just $5 a night, Ellendale Pool provides a magnificent base camp for exploring nearby Greenough and Geraldton too.

You can climb the rocky river's edge to where the creek feeds the pool, or paddle in silence at dawn, feeling the presence, perhaps, of the dreaming serpent Bimarra who Yamaji people believe sleeps under a cave at the pool. Sunsets ignite the glowing red-and-white tinted cliffs, so if you head out to explore for the day, be sure to be back in time to watch the spectacle from your camp chair.

A waterhole this big and full is bound to have a history, and around camp, you can read about the refuge that Ellendale Pool has offered Yamaji people and, more recently, the explorers, pioneers and settlers whose stock depended upon its waters.

Located 50km southeast of Geraldton and close to the coast at Greenough, Ellendale is a beautiful, spacious, low-cost camp for nature-lovers keen to spend time exploring the region. From here, you can head to South Greenough to catch crays at Flat Rocks or launch your boat to fish the sheltered river mouth at Cape Burney. A visit to Greenough Wildlife Park is highly recommended for kids, as is a tour through Greenough Central Historic Area (with a free tasting of Copperhead Road Distillery rums for the over 18s).

For many years now, when the weather warms up, Ellendale Pool has suffered the seasonal appearance of amoebas that cause the potentially fatal amoebic meningitis. This happens when the water warms to 24°C or higher, so swimming is strictly at your own risk. To play it safe, take to the water only in the cool winter months and if you decide to swim, keep your head (especially your nose) well above water.

Camping facilities are excellent and include toilets, cold outdoor showers, sheltered picnic tables, free gas barbecues, a playground, dump point and non-potable water. Campfires are permitted from April to September, and fees are just $5 per campsite, payable via an honesty box on site. To get there, turn off the Brand Highway north of Greenough onto Yamaji Drive and continue for about 30km. The final 100m of gravel is fine for 2WD vehicles and caravans.

01 Camp right by the Greenough River's edge in this Kimberley-inspired landscape.

COALSEAM 16/100 ☐
CONSERVATION PARK

01

Camp in a sea of everlasting daisies and discover ancient marine fossils.

When winter rains fall, dazzling displays of daisies blanket this rugged outback sanctuary, carpeting the Irwin River's banks with the papery pom pom everlasting daisies the Yamaji people call birriny-birriny. So popular is this destination for its wildflowers and fossils that, from late July to October, stays here are limited to just three days to cope with the crowds.

But this spectacular conservation park almost didn't exist at all. Back in 1846,

three British explorers, the Gregory brothers, discovered coal seams along the Irwin River. Sheep farmers had their eyes on the surrounding countryside too, but Coalseam was spared thanks to the tricky-to-mine coal and a rugged landscape too tough for sheep.

Today, this little pocket of wild showcases some incredible ancient marine fossils embedded in striking cliffs layered with ancient sandstone, granite and coal. To see them, walk 400 metres from the picnic area at Riverbend, or drive to the fossil picnic area and walk to the opposite riverbank. Follow the loop trail to Irwin Lookout (560m) and spot wedge-tailed eagles and peregrine falcons soaring above the riverbed and carpets of everlastings (Rhodanthe chlorocephala subsp. rosea). Known to the Yamiji people as ugudungu, these flowers, which feel papery to touch, fill fields of the most breathtaking pink, yellow and white, and can also be found en mass at Morawa and Depot Hill. The Everlastings' daisies have become quite a popular cut flower in the floristry industry, due to their ability to dry well and keep their colour for up to a year.

Accessible by 2WD vehicles and located 100km east of Geraldton or a 30-minute drive from Mingenew, the park is close enough to visit in a day, but a favourite amongst self-sufficient campers who stake out Miners Camp and explore old mine shafts nearby.

The Plateau Loop Trail begins here, too, winding beneath rare eucalypts to a lofty ridge for breathtaking views across the valley (3.2km).

Unpowered campsites suit all sizes of rigs and come with barbecues, picnic tables and toilets. Bring drinking water and pay fees upon arrival to the on-site camp host over winter ($11 adults, $7 concessions and $3 per child aged 5 – 16 years). When you visit, pack a telescope because Mingenew Shire is a radio quiet zone, which promises some of the clearest stargazing in the state.

01 Pom Pom Everlastings growing en masse in Morawa.

02 Fields of Everlastings. Stunning to see and papery to touch.

ST FRANCIS 77/100 ☐
XAVIER CATHEDRAL

Is this the best Roman cathedral outside of Rome?

With towering stone architecture and a startling candy-striped interior, this show-stopping masterpiece is one of a kind and the most significant work of celebrated architect Monsignor Hawes. Fronted by a labyrinth that mimics the one in Notre Dame's Chartres Cathedral and topped with a towering 27-bell carillon that rings out each night, it hosts hugely popular $5 tours and has a world-class interpretive centre too.

Opened in 2016, the Monsignor Hawes Heritage Centre rounds off all cathedral tours with interactive displays and artefacts that showcase the life's work of this famous priest and architect. Inside the cathedral itself, guides lead you down into a stunning underground crypt and reveal the thinking behind that extraordinary orange-and-grey striped mosaic baptismal pool. Tours run on Sundays, Mondays and Wednesdays at 2.30 pm and Fridays at 4 pm, and outside the cathedral, there are flower gardens to explore, a café and gift shop.

Heritage-listed and flawlessly restored, St Francis Xavier Cathedral was built between 1916 and 1938, and its 27 bells ring out across Geraldton all day long. Visit after dark at around 7.30 pm when the cathedral is lit up, and Australia's largest carillon rings the bells in poignant, harmonious tunes. The cathedral is open from 7.30 am to 5.30 pm daily, and the heritage centre from 10 am to 4 pm.

HMAS SYDNEY II ¹⁸/₁₀₀ ☐
MEMORIAL

Catch sunrise and commemorate Australia's worst maritime tragedy.

The sinking of the HMAS Sydney II by the German ship HSK Kormoran on November 19, 1941, remains the most tragic naval loss in Australia's history. On that night, 645 Australian men – the entire crew of this celebrated naval light cruiser – were drowned 120km off the WA coastline. 315 of the Kormoran's 393 men survived the brief engagement, to then be held as prisoners of war.

After decades of searching, the wrecks of both ships were finally located in 2008, 22km apart in 2.5km of water, 120km west of Steep Point. Finally, the hotly debated question of how a modified merchant vessel like the Kormoran could defeat the fast, purpose-built warship Sydney, could be answered.

Today, the hilltop HMAS Sydney II Memorial commemorates the battle; its silver shroud of 645 stainless steel seagulls crowning the scene with a 'Dome of Souls', inspired by the old seafarers' belief that seagulls carry the souls of men lost at sea. A bronze sculpture of the ever-patient Waiting Woman gazes out across the ocean, while in the Pool of Remembrance, a seagull's wingtip marks the location where the HMAS Sydney II went down.

A nearby Wall of Remembrance remembers the names of men lost in this deadly battle. Arrive at first light to watch one of the most memorial sunrises on the coast, or join a free walking tour, conducted daily at 10.30 am. You'll find it on Gummer Ave. Learn more at **hmassydneymemorialgeraldton. com.au**.

THE TIN HEADS ¹⁹/100 □

Chart modern history with biscuit tins? Meet the Tin Heads.

If you told us that 12,200 decorative tea, biscuit and chocolate tins might stack up to a quirky history of the modern world, we'd have been highly sceptical. But Geraldton locals Margaret and Robert Gaston's incredible collection has proven us wrong.

Back in 2005, the couple had just 35 tins of sentimental value, like the tin that held bike parts when Robert was a kid and the first tin of Peters Ice cream the couple bought after they were married. Today their collection dates back to the 1850s and hails from around the world.

Some are obscure and some famously recognisable, like their black and orange Weetbix tins, and tins for Twinings Tea and ANZAC biscuits too.

Robert and Margaret are generous storytellers, regaling visitors with yarns about each precious piece in their collection. They generally open their museum every second Sunday of the month, but you can make private appointments by calling **0428 383 208**. It's free to visit, but you are welcome to make a donation to the pair's favourite charity, the Heart Foundation. You'll find the Gaston's property just north of Geraldton at 72 Beatie Road, Waggrakine.

LEARN

Bringing its proud history to life, Geraldton takes many travellers by surprise, hijacking travel itineraries with an excess of museums, historical adventures and cultural fun.

Some are quirky (try Northampton's Sewing Machine Museum), others will regale you with pioneering flashbacks or have you sitting like a shipwreck survivor on a replica 1600s-era longboat. These three are great ways to start.

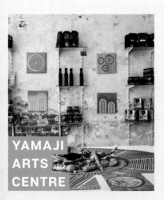

YAMAJI ARTS CENTRE

MUSEUM OF GERALDTON

LUCIA ARCADIA

The Yamaji Art Centre is a vibrant, creative hub, which nurtures a rich network of ceramists, painters, basket weavers and jewellery makers. 100% Aboriginal owned and operated, the centre welcomes visitors to its gallery, get messy in its workshops, or accompany resident artists on tours that end with bush tucker and didgeridoo performances. The gallery sells canvases, wearable art, clothing and emu eggs too. yamajiart.com

Famed for its Shipwrecks Gallery that regales travellers with seafaring tales and archaeological riches from four Dutch shipwrecks, Geraldton's museum is one of the best in the west. Learn about the mutiny on Batavia and how the crew survived after the Zeewijk went down. From Great Depths reveals the wreck of HMAS Sydney II. Entry is free, and permanent exhibitions showcase Yamaji culture and local history. museum.wa.gov.au

A micro-farmer, artist and sustainable florist, Lucia Arcadia has gained a reputation for her great knowledge and deep love for wildflowers. Growing up on her grandparents' farm, she'd roam the property in search of all kinds of wild botanical blooms. These days Lucia micro-farms wildflowers, transforming them into floral-inspired art. Throughout this chapter and others, she's detailed her favourite flowers. facebook.com/ oliveandmustard

Escape the coast for views, food and historical wonders.

The Moresby Range rises high above the Chapman Valley, its flat-topped mesas flanked by everlasting daisies, historical villages and a growing number of savvy eateries too. All of it appeals enormously to travellers seeking scenic wanders away from the coast, and the first stop for foodies is Burnt Barrel.

Head here hungry to sate your appetite, Kansas-style, on spicy, 16-hour smoked meats, 'ugly crust' pies, and tantalising veg, vegan and kids meals (try the barbecued pulled jackfruit burger).

If you need to walk off the meal, there's a top little nature trail at nearby Nandon, famed for sightings of endangered Carnaby's black cockatoos and ringtail possums. Everlasting daisies carpet the roadsides everywhere during the wildflower season and are particularly prolific at Naraling Hall en route to Yuna, and at Wandana Reserve further east.

So historically rich is this region, it's got its own scenic drive back in time: the 100km-long Chapman Valley Heritage Trail. Highlights include a wander through the museum at Nandon (entry by donation) and a visit to Our Lady of Fatima Catholic Church (and convent), the work of world-famous architect and priest Monsignor John Hawes.

Easily accessible to Geraldton, Northampton and the campground at Coronation Beach, you could tour Chapman Valley in a day, but if you want to soak it up a bit longer, two top little campgrounds at Fig Tree Crossing and Yuna provide basic facilities for self-sufficient travellers ($10/adult).

EAT

Big enough to have a genuine food scene but small enough that it's not pretentious, Geraldton is one fine place to dine.

You might be eating the best toasted sandwich within sight of the sea, cracking a fresh-off-the-boat rock lobster, or ordering a boutique beer in a centuries-old pub. If you need a good meal, we can't recommend these three places highly enough.

JAFFLE SHACK

PIPER LANE CAFE

THE PROVINCIAL

Few things are as simple and satisfying as a properly toasted sandwich enjoyed with a great view over the water. There are two Jaffle Shacks in town, but the locals love the one on Foreshore Drive, overlooking the north end of Geraldton Beach. Grab a coffee, try the famous mi goreng jaffle, have a game of noughts and crosses, and tap into Geraldton's Free City Wi-Fi while you wait. Afterwards, stroll down to the free waterpark to cool off. jaffleshack.com.au

Stroll along Marine Terrace and there's no shortage of great spots to eat or drink. A highlight, though, is Piper Lane. You can also walk from the beach or waterpark through an archway of greenery to discover this little laneway cafe. Fully licensed with a good wine menu, all-day brekkie, and a charming little setting, it's a hidden gem in the heart of town where locals flock at all times of the day. Grab a seat in the laneway under the morning sun. piperlanecafe.com.au

From the outside, it looks like any unassuming regional pub, but step inside and you'll discover the sandstone brickwork, edgy-art decor, hand-crafted pizza and tapas menu, and live entertainment that set this place apart. This is the go-to place in Geraldton for everything from an easy takeaway to dinner and late-night drinks. If you're not keen on dining in, takeaway is available Tuesday to Sunday evenings. Find it at 167 Marine Terrace. theprovincial.com.au

01

Go where the wreath flowers bloom.

This weird and wonderful floral phenomenon blooms briefly at the end of wildflower season, luring flower-chasers west onto the red Geraldton sandplains. September seems to be the best month to see the utterly unique wreath lechenaultia flowers (lechenaultia macrantha) that colour roadsides in frilly pink-and-red clusters around the historical town of Pindar. To reach a favourite viewing area, head for Pindar (128km west of Geraldton), turn left at the Old Pindar Hotel down Beringarra-Pindar Rd and continue 10km out of town (you can't miss them).

Established in 1901 on sheep grazing and gold, Pindar's heyday has long since passed, but the heritage-listed Old Pindar Hotel remains a popular place for lunch. Now run as a tearoom and café, the hotel's home-baked scones have a bit of a following. Find their opening times and get updates on wreath flowers in bloom at facebook.com/oldpindarhotel.

of the year. When no other nectar-producing plant is in flower, the Banksia prionotes supplies nutrients for many different animals.

Nearby Mullewa is all about wildflowers too, famous for its annual wildflower show and the orchids, everlastings, grevilleas and hakeas that carpet the region. Visit in August to catch the show and to walk through wildflowers on the Mullewa Bushland Trail Drive. It sets out from Mullewa's scenic lookout and provides insight into the area's Indigenous culture, too (2.4km, 40 minutes).

If you are here between February and April, lookout for the acorn or orange banksia (Banksia prionotes). Not only is this flower beautiful and long-lasting, but it also has a vital role to play in the Midwest ecosystem. It provides the only source of nectar in the Avon Wheatbelt during some of the hottest months

Mullewa's other great attraction is impossible to miss: a stunning creation by celebrated architect Monsignor John Hawes (of St Francis Xavier Cathedral fame), who fused Romanesque and Gothic architectural features in building the distinctive Our Lady of Mount Carmel Church. With its towering white domes, stone pillars and even a gargoyle, it's an unexpected site in this little outback town and rates as one of the finest of Monsignor Hawes' 29 Australian masterpieces.

01 Look for wreath flowers growing in clusters along the dusty roadsides outside of Pindar.

02 The historic Old Pindar Hotel is a must-stop for its tearoom and accommodation.

03 September is the best time for sighting the unique wreath flower.

OAKABELLA ²²/₁₀₀ ☐
HOMESTEAD AND TEAROOMS

Discover Oakabella Gorge and tour one of WA's most haunted properties.

With a pioneering past that stretches back to the 1850s, it's little wonder that Oakabella Homestead has a few secrets in its closets. Much more than a unique place to camp and eat, Oakabella serves up ghostly Homestead Tours and sunset wanders through Oakabella Gorge that weave in Yamaji Dreamtime storytelling, bush tucker, fresh-baked damper and didgeridoo playing around the campfire.

Exploring Oakabella's more recent pioneering past, Caretaker Loretta leads tours through the 13-room homestead and the adjacent Buttress Barn that houses the museum, revealing a glimpse of what daily life might have been like for hardy early settlers and regaling you with some spooky supernatural stories too.

The tearooms are licensed and open daily, and if you're not easily spooked, the campground is pet-friendly and costs $12 (adults) and $5 for kids (under 5s stay for free). Visit from September to October when the countryside is coloured by fields of bright blooming canola and natural wildflowers. You'll find it 35km north of Geraldton on Starling Road, signposted off the North West Coastal Highway. oakabellahomestead.com.au

CORONATION ²³/₁₀₀ ☐
BEACH

Brave the waves at this world-class kite and windsurfing spot.

Known as the Fremantle Doctor – or simply 'The Doctor' – the blustery sea breeze that revives Perth City on stifling summer days is felt right along the Coral Coast too. It's strongest over summer when the difference between sea and land temperatures is greatest, and that's when the kitesurfing and windsurfing action get gloriously hectic at Coronation Beach.

The conditions here are world-class, with plenty of swell whipped up by summer's predominantly south-westerly winds, thrilling wave riders most of all. There's a small flat zone here for much of the year, but when The Doctor blows, sometimes pushing gusts to 25-30 knots, beginners quickly exit into the shallows. On calm mornings (especially over the less windy months in spring and autumn), you can swim and SUP off the wide, sandy beach.

Coronation Beach is equally popular as a beachfront haven for self-sufficient campers who stake out breezy seaside sites over the cool winter months. It's great for fishing and surfing too, and the scenic, sandy campsites are affordable at $10 per adult and $8 for pensioners (kids under 16 years stay for free).

Here, facilities are basic but include toilets, barbecues, a dump point, rubbish bins and a shower room (bring water and a solar bag). The camp is pet-friendly, and there's a campground host on-site, but no bookings are taken, so arrive early to grab a great site over winter.

HORROCKS BEACH ²⁴/₁₀₀ □

White sand, turquoise lagoon and a timber fishing jetty. Need we say more?

This photogenic beach haven is an award-winning spot, celebrated as one of the West Coast's most beautiful beaches. Fringed by a colourful coastline of beach shacks and a giant cirque of reef that cradles a stunning turquoise lagoon, Horrocks might be just another pretty bay if it weren't for the exemplary angling, paddling, surfing and diving that takes place here.

Conditions are perfect for water sports from March to October (or June to November if you come to catch crays). The timber jetty that stretches seaward serves up catches of whiting, skipjack and tailor, and incongruously, provides an irresistible jump-off platform for the young at heart to scatter the fish too. Anglers and surfers both favour Bowes River Mouth and the outer reef, where the waves are consistent and catches of snapper and dhufish reliable. Great flocks of waterbirds gather at the river mouth, too: eagles and ospreys, pelicans, black swans, herons and egrets, all colouring vibrant coastal scenes.

You can launch your boat off Horrocks Beach or 4WD north along the soft,

01 Swim, SUP or fish from the pristine waters of Horrocks' beach.

02 Catch whiting, skipjack and tailor straight off the picturesque jetty.

sandy track to three isolated campsites at Little Bay, where there's more great fishing and good surf. Let your tyres down and pack a SUP or kayak for exploring the bay, plus camping gear and plenty of drinking water because this little gem is pretty difficult to leave.

For showers and power, head back to the Horrocks Beach Caravan Park or bed down at Horrocks Beachside Cottages or one of the BnBs in town. There are a few places to dine, but the most memorable eats come wrapped in paper from the General Store, whose takeaway fish and chips command a heap of praise.

If you're looking for ways to bookend lazy days by the sea, drive to the whale watching lookout above town to spot migrating humpbacks over the winter months. You'll find it on the left-hand side of Horrocks Road as you enter town. Continue on to the Bowes River Road junction to reach Willigully Caves, where sandstone overhangs protect galleries etched by the Nanda people describing their stories, lessons and values. Motifs here were once used on message sticks and serve as a reminder to visitors of the sacredness of this coastline to Indigenous peoples.

HOUTMAN-
ABROLHOS ISLANDS

01

A tropical cluster of faraway isles where life is truly wild!

There might not be palm trees and coconuts, but these faraway isles are a wild, tropical wonderland, girthed by coral reefs and inhabited by lobster fishers and the centuries-old graves of shipwreck survivors. Bathed by the warm-flowing Leeuwin Current, vibrant reefs nurture Australian sea lions, green sea turtles and bottlenose dolphins, and western rock lobsters are found in numbers that make Geraldton famous.

The snorkelling and diving are world-class (and the best on the west coast), and fishing charters to the Abrolhos Islands routinely reel in coral trout, pink snapper, dhufish and incredible catches of baldchin groper. Located about 60km west of Geraldton, where tropical and temperate waters meet, the Abrolhos Islands boast impossibly turquoise seas and the kind of shimmering white sand beaches that only come from coral.

Balmy water temperatures never dip below 20°C, even in winter, putting this island group firmly on the bucket list of divers, snorkellers and surfers too. Part of what makes the Abrolhos so special is how tricky it is to get here. Daytrippers can jump aboard a scenic flight out of Geraldton or Kalbarri (preferably with ground exploring included) or spend 80 minutes on the fast ferry (abrolhosadventures.com.au). Live-aboard fishing and diving charters indulge your passions for longer, and since there's no visitor accommodation or camping on the islands, only private boats with their own beds onboard make it this far west.

In stark contrast to the rich underwater world, the islands themselves are more 'desert' than 'isle'. Lobster fishing shacks occupy 22 of the islands, but almost nothing blooms here, and the landscape is so harsh that the local tamar wallabies have evolved to drink seawater.

It's a realisation that must have shattered shipwreck survivors of the Batavia back in 1629 after they managed to make it to shore. If the shipwreck experience that drowned 40 passengers wasn't bad enough, what happened next amounts to the darkest slice of Australia's entire exploration history: mutiny, mass murder, sexual slavery and the first legal executions documented to take place on Australian shores. Embroiled in this horror story, soldier Wiebbe Hayes waged battle with the mutineers in a bid to free enslaved survivors, and his fort on Wallabi Island survives as the oldest European building in the country. The Abrolhos has snagged more than

90 ships on its reefy 'graveyards', and there are remnants of burial sites and a survivors' camp on Beacon Island.

Despite its tragic human history, this refuge of biodiversity supports more than 90 species of seabird, and Australian sea lions covet the coral beaches off Peos Island. From July to October, humpback whales migrate past, and on land, you'll spot nocturnal tammar wallabies (Macropus eugenii) at dusk and dawn.

The best time to visit the islands is from February to June or September to October, when light wind conditions make the journey most comfortable. If you are planning to surf, monitor conditions from May to September. When you go, download 'The Abrolhos Islands Information Guide' for advice on boating, fishing, dive sites and background history (fish.wa.gov.au).

If you can't reach the Abrolhos, sail instead aboard Geraldton's Batavia Longboat – a replica of the boat that ferried shipwreck survivors to the barren shores of Beacon Island in 1629. Public sailing days are free and promise to regale you with harrowing tales as you trim the sails or steer the boat. Sailing takes place most Sundays from the Batavia Marina at the Museum of Geraldton (donations welcome). Find out more at facebook.com/batavialongboat.

01 No boat? No worries. Jump on the fast ferry from Geraldton. Day tours from $250 per adult, $200 for kids under 12.

KALBARRI

Sandwiched between plunging sea cliffs and a dramatic river gorge, this wild coastal hamlet provides grand opportunities to play.

Kalbarri locals rave about the top surf break at Jakes, the wintertime wildflowers that fringe their favourite walking trails, and the paddling, the pelicans and the secret curls of sand that nestle between crumbling sea cliffs close to town.

An unrelenting swell sculpts this coastline, lofty lookouts poise above natural rock bridges and cavernous amphitheatres, and dolphins ride the breakers far below. Just inland where the mighty Murchison River winds to the sea, a sandstone window in the rock frames Kalbarri's most famous scene, and a pair of skywalks suspend you over the abyss, dangling high above the rocky river gorge.

Elsewhere around town, wildflowers colour plains studded with lolly-pink lakes, paddlers and anglers meet in the eddying calm between the river and the sea, and off-roaders escape along sandy tracks to the unforgettable Lucky Bay.

NATURE'S WINDOW

MURCHISON HOUSE

Z BEND

MURCHISON RIVER

KALBARRI

JACQUES BEACH

KALBARRI
NATIONAL PARK

NATURAL BRIDGE

YALLABATHARRA

LUCKY BAY

HUTT LAGOON

PORT GREGORY

LYNTON

Window to the world. Nature's Window, Kalbarri National Park.

With all this wonder, is it any surprise that Kalbarri's early residents tackled 500km of boggy, sandy and rutted tracks just to holiday here?

Like the tin-shack settlements at Wedge and Grey to the south, it was anglers who kick-started Kalbarri in the 1940s, lured to this faraway coastline by warm weather, carefree living and their next big catch. Back then, it was called 'Mouth of the Murch', a colloquial name that persisted well into the 1960s. But this pristine wilderness did not go unnoticed, and even in the late 1940s, the WA government was toying with the idea of throwing national park boundaries around the entire, wondrous landscape.

Whether it was Kalbarri's remote location, the desirable size of its ample harbour, or simply public sentiment, this tin-shack settlement survived and flourished within the heart of a great wilderness that's today protected as Kalbarri National Park. According to historian and Parks and Wildlife officer Rory Chappel, the town and the national park that bears its name developed symbiotically, and they both benefit from the annual influx of tourists drawn to the park's diverse natural scenes.

Here, where the Outback meets the sea, critically endangered species find sanctuary in a rugged landscape that the Nanda people call Wutumalu. Their Dreamtime story tells how the rainbow serpent created the Murchison River gorge, winding downstream and awakening ancestors en route to the sea. At the ocean, she was met by the evil spirit Gabba Gabba, and fled north, carving out the mighty Zuytdorp Cliffs and churning up treacherous seas that characterise the coastline at Steep Point and Shark Bay.

Kalbarri has come a long way from its early days as a far-flung fishing village, but locals still retain a deep love for this rugged coastal wilderness and all the ways it allows them to explore.

STAY

After long beachy days spent surfing Kalbarri's reef breaks and hiking coastal trails, travellers slink back after sunset to rinse, eat and sleep.

Accommodation choices in this laidback holiday hamlet are thankfully low-rise and plentiful: everything from private seaside retreats and boutique B&Bs, to simple beach shacks, campsites and budget backpacker hostels. Bear in mind that Perth's holiday escapees swarm Kalbarri during school breaks (it's only a half-day's drive north), so book well ahead or time your trip for late July through August, when wildflowers are still in bloom, and the kids are back at their desks.

LINGA LONGA, LYNTON STATION

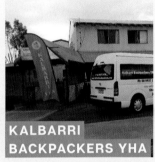

KALBARRI BACKPACKERS YHA

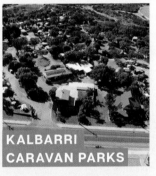

KALBARRI CARAVAN PARKS

Close to Lynton Convict Hiring Depot's ruins, this working sheep and cattle station provides Kalbarri's quieter, out-of-town option. There's 4WD access to the beach, and you can take a self-guided tour through Lynton Station's heritage-listed homestead, which dates back to 1853. Book campsites here (from $15 per person, kids $10), or the station's simple farm cottage sleeps a family of four at $165 a night. Call ahead to book – **0438 916 202.**

A central choice for budget stays, Kalbarri's backpacker hub is within easy walking distance of the foreshore, where you can grab breakfast at Black Rock Café, hit the beach and join the daily Pelican Feeding session. There's a mix of dorm and double rooms (from $30 a night) and a pool, and the manager is a long-time local who'll offer great insight and tips for planning the best adventures in town. **kalbarribackpackers. com.**

Just across the road from the pelican feeding and the mouth of the Murchison River, this holiday park is a favourite amongst self-sufficient campers and caravanners. It's family-run, and campsites start at $31 (unpowered). **murcp.com.**
If you are looking for a pool, try Kalbarri Anchorage Holiday Park instead, overlooking the Murchison River from $30/night. **kalbarrianchorage. com.au.**

Touch crumbling stone cells etched with the names of convict prisoners.

Preserving a rare slice of the west's convict past, these 160-year-old ruins stud the hillside on the scenic drive into Kalbarri. It was established as a labour depot back in 1853 to house around 30 trusted, ticket-of-leave convicts, whose cheap physical labour was needed to run the burgeoning Geraldton Lead Mine and on pastoral operations around Port Gregory.

The best workers were quickly snapped up to work the farms, the mine and (controversially) to build assistant superintendent Captain Henry Sanford's private homestead. But with workers kept busy, the depot itself was slow to build, and the tent city that housed prisoners for years was, by all reports, a place of mistreatment, corruption and illness.

remains of the old barracks, built to sleep 80 men in hammocks, plus the hospital, magistrate's quarters, lockup and a cemetery. The site, located on Port Gregory Road between Northampton and Kalbarri, is open at all times and free to enter.

From the depot site, walk or drive up the road to Lynton Station to take a tour through Captain Sanford's far superior, convict-built homestead, reportedly built using unauthorised convict labour and depot stores, and impressively restored today. Entry here is free too (although donations are welcomed), and across the road, the modern-day Lynton Station welcomes campers with powered and unpowered sites, and rents a self-contained cottage.

Only once Sanford resigned and convict masons were sent north from Perth did construction speed up, but the depot was barely finished when it was closed in December 1956 due to transport problems and harsh living conditions.

Today you can take a self-guided wander around the crumbling stone buildings, some of which are etched with inmates' initials, scratched into their cell walls. There's plenty of interpretive signage to guide you around what

01 The old barracks, built to sleep 80 men, was completed in 1853.

02 The lockup, which was used for short term imprisonment.

01

Lolly-pink, shimmering and very Insta-worthy.

It's home to the world's largest microalgae production plant and lots of brine shrimp, but that's not what will blow you away about this lolly-pink spectacle. Got your camera ready?

Shimmering in ever-changing shades of hot pink, lavender and lilac that shift with the weather, Hutt Lagoon has many guises. What makes it bewitching is the microalgae Dunaliella salina, which colours the lake with bright beta-carotene (just like carrots). The time of day, the amount of cloud cover overhead and how well the algae are blooming all affect the lake's exact colour. The natural pink hue waxes and wanes, but locals say that the most vibrant colours come from clear skies and intense sunshine, seen from 10am to 2pm, and again at sunset too.

Quite apart from being a stellar tourist attraction, this remarkable rosy sea produces a rich harvest of beta-carotene and is mined for its salt too. You'll start to catch glimpses of the pink as you drive north along Port Gregory Road from the Lynton Convict Hiring Depot. The road to Port Gregory (George Grey Drive) leads you close to the water's edge, and it's worth pushing on to this sleepy seaside town to fish, swim and beachcomb, or to stay for the night so that you can easily catch sunset down by the lake.

Sheltered by an extensive line of reef close to shore, Port Gregory's tranquil lagoon smooths the way for beginner swimmers, and you can fish off the jetty, launch a boat and go waterskiing. There's also a neat little caravan park.

Continuing on into Kalbarri, you'll pass plenty of pull-offs and access tracks that cut through the scrub to the lake, but you'd do well to walk these as they quickly turn boggy. Hutt Lagoon looks incredible from the sky, too (hello drone shot), and scenic flights from Kalbarri and Geraldton are a popular way to capture the enormity of this strawberry-milk inland sea, juxtaposed against the deep blue Indian Ocean that runs alongside.

01 George Grey Drive runs alongside Hutt Lagoon, allowing for multiple vantage points.

02 Beware of razor sharp rocks beneath the surface.

03 The lagoon is harvested for its beta-carotene and salt.

01

Camp on the beach, snorkel the lagoon and hit the dunes.

Meandering past ramshackle beach shacks en route to Lucky Bay, 4WD travellers make a beeline for the sea, climbing soft sand dunes in search of secluded spots to fish and swim. A long reef stretches close to shore, snagging the waves and sheltering Lucky Bay's blissfully calm lagoon for snorkelling, diving and spearfishing fun. Catches of crayfish are common, and you'll likely share the enormous lagoon with kiteboarders and windsurfers when the afternoon breeze kicks in.

Surfers find their nirvana on the break to the south of the bay, and all along this long, remote shoreline, 4WD travellers park up on the sand, shake out camp chairs and fishing rods and wait for spectacular, watery sunsets. Expect catches of herring, whiting, tailor and dart, plus mulloway off the beach and all kinds of reef species off the tip of the reef as you head north to Wagoes.

What Lucky Bay offers in droves is pure, unadulterated freedom, and for lovers of self-sufficient camping, few spots beat the scenes on offer here. You can camp anywhere on this coastal stretch (provided you have a

02

toilet onboard), but there's a proper campground behind the dunes with 2WD access and basic facilities like picnic shelters, toilets, fire rings, rubbish bins and a dump point. Sites here cost $15 per vehicle, per night (EFTPOS available), paid on-site to the camp host. You can't book ahead, but there's plenty of room, and if your itinerary is loose, you can stay for up to 28 days.

To really explore and navigate the sandy tracks that lead on to the beach, you'll need a 4WD with soft tyres (try 15psi). This is how you'll find that perfect fishing spot and a private place to swim, or scale the massive sand dunes for endless sea views and incredible drone shots. If you head into the dunes to sandboard and explore, beware of the huge drop-offs that loom suddenly, and attach a sand flag to your vehicle too.

Not to be confused with the other Lucky Bay in Esperance, this Lucky Bay is located about a 35-minute drive south of Kalbarri (47km). Turn west off George Grey Road onto Balline Road and continue past the shacks at Half Way Bay to the campground and the beach. Stop at the rangers station on your way in to pay for your stay. Now run by WA's Department of Parks and Wildlife, Lucky Bay's campground is pet-friendly and permits campfires in designated fire rings or portable containers only, so bring plenty of firewood, drinking water and an air compressor for your tyres.

01 The beach lagoon is the perfect spot to snorkel in crystal-clear, calm waters.

02 Enjoy prime, beach-front camping for only $15 per vehicle, per night.

BIGURDA TRAIL 29/100 □

01

Hike along the lofty edge of Kalbarri's dramatically sculpted sea cliffs.

This sky-high seaside trail carves a wildly scenic path, skirting 100m above the unrelenting Indian Ocean along the sandstone cliffs it pummels. Millions of years of wave action have transformed this coastline into a series of eye-catching, multi-hued landmarks. Today, overhung lookouts gaze across at the Shellhouse, Grandstand Rock Gorge and Island Rock, standing sentry beneath the cliffs.

The Bigurda Trail links them all, stretching for 8km between Eagle Gorge and Natural Bridge, and named for the mobs of common wallaroos (or euros) that the Nanda people call bigurda. The hike takes 3-5 hours to complete (one-way), and although you can access all of its grand sights by car, walking the trail whisks you beyond the often crowded lookouts for invigorating vistas of dolphins riding the breakers. Humpback whales breach out to sea during their June to November migration, and a top tip for spotters is that they cruise much closer to the coast on their south-bound journey towards year's end.

Unless you want to walk the trail twice, you'll need to shuffle two cars or leave your bike at the end for the 8.8km cycle back, but it's easy enough to find other hikers and travellers to hitch with. Ordinarily, walkers set out from Eagle Gorge (off George Grey Drive) and walk south to Natural Bridge, but when the wind is blowing hard from the south, tackle this trail in reverse so that the wind is at your back.

From Eagle Gorge, a short trail leads down to rock pools by the beach, past ancient skolithos straws that hang from the surrounding sandstone. Burrowed by ancient creatures and filled with sand and fossilised, the skolithos are so similar to ones found in Antarctica that scientists believe it once joined this part of the coast during the Devonian period when Australia was still part of Gondwana.

Just over halfway into the walk, lookouts over the Shellhouse and Grandstand Rock Gorge elevate you to the highest vantage points along the trail, and beyond here, the cliffs become sheer and other-worldly. By the time you reach Island Rock, a boardwalk paves the way to the enigmatic, eroded Natural Bridge at Castle Cove and trail's end.

Rated Class 3, the Bigurda Trail is gravelly, mostly flat and moderate, but expect uneven sections and rocks and plenty of distractions from the swooping eagles, bigurdas (euro kangaroos), and in winter, great blooms of national park-protected wildflowers.

01 The view from the lookout, overlooking the Natural Bridge.

02 The 3-5 hour walk offers stunning scenery and fantastic whalewatching.

RAINBOW VALLEY, ³⁰/₁₀₀ ☐ MUSHROOM ROCK AND POT ALLEY

Clifftop trails, secluded beaches and lofty sunset lookouts.

Rainbow Valley shimmers in the mist, the incoming Indian Ocean swell crashing along its sea cliffs and sending skywards kaleidoscopic, salty sprays to colour the sunset vista. All around, there are rainbows in the rock, too: vibrant layers from an ancient seabed revealed in ever-changing hues of purple and orange, set aglow as the setting sun slowly turns back towards the sea.

From Pot Alley north to Rainbow Valley, secluded beaches and trails lure explorers to the coast, on less ambitious excursions than the worthy Bigurda Trail, but no less stunning. A leisurely meander sets out towards Mushroom Rock, looping past wildly eroded cliffs to this creatively named formation.

There's much to learn about this coastline's geology and biology as you venture on towards Rainbow Valley. Tackling the class 4 loop takes about one to two hours (3km return), and you can set out from carparks at Mushroom Rock or Rainbow Valley, both signposted off George Grey Drive, a short drive south of Kalbarri's foreshore.

Another sunset spot that few travellers find, Pot Alley Beach is easy to reach at day's end. From the carpark (signposted off George Grey Drive south of town), a stepped trail descends 200m through a sandstone gully to a secluded little beach waiting just for you. It takes just 10 minutes to reach, even when you're loaded up with sunset drinks, snacks and a blanket for the sand.

EAT

Kalbarri's outdoorsy, surfing vibe permeates the way people spend their days, but more so, it shapes the way people eat here too.

Serving up more than fish and chips with a view, restaurants, cafes, and food trucks deliver ever-changing menus of tapas and fresh seafood, raw food, fine dining and plenty of spice and fire! If you wonder where the locals like to spend their money, head to one of these three spots and meet them yourself.

FINLAY'S KALBARRI

They brew their own beer and cider, let you bring pets, and encourage kids to play in their boats. Oh, and they serve seafood, locally caught in Kalbarri (try the cockles teamed with a Jacques on Point IPA). When the weather's great, the beer garden is perfect for sunny day drinks, and on wintry nights the campfire is lit. Finlay's has been a cornerstone meeting place for more than 30 years. Open noon Friday to Sunday and for dinners on Wednesday and Thursday nights too. **finlayskalbarri.com.au.**

BEAN DRIFTING

For the best coffee in town, you're going to have to head out of it, following Red Bluff Road to Jacques Point, where this quaint little coffee cart serves up early morning brews. The coastal views provide a pretty mesmerising backdrop as you sit and sip and wake up with the waves. They sell bakery goodies and light snacks and, most importantly, darn good brews. Find them most days between 7:30 and 11:30 am, especially over the winter months. **facebook.com/ beandrifting.**

WILD OCEAN INDONESIAN

This place gets wild local praise for its authentic Indonesian fare – beef rendang, sweet potato noodle spring rolls and tempura prawns – sold from a food truck, usually parked down on the Foreshore. Follow your nose down Grey Street to the Fisherman's Wharf, arriving in plenty of time to place your order and dine al fresco in the park as the sun goes down. The truck opens for business on Friday, Saturday and Sunday evenings, from about 5 pm to 7:30 pm. Call ahead on **0400 201 131.**

Snorkel the uber-blue rock pools and find Australia's first European settlement.

Bright moon wrasse and raccoon butterfly fish flourish in the Blue Holes' pristine, protected pools, colouring this unlikely snorkelling spot on Kalbarri's usually choppy coastline. Sheltered by a line of reef that holds back the low tide, these coral-fringed rock pools provide sanctuary for 70 species of fish, along with western rock lobsters and sponges, banded hair shrimps and beds of oysters – all of it protected for snorkellers and divers to explore.

Uber-blue and impossible to stay out of, the Blue Holes stretch for 240 metres along the coast between the river mouth and Jakes Point and look as amazing underwater as they do from above. The sandy beach is shimmering and white, and the best part for beginner swimmers is that at low tide, these pools are amongst the most protected on the coast, so don your mask and get wet! The Blue Holes are signposted off Red Bluff Road (aka George Grey Drive), just north of Jakes and Red Bluff Beach.

Just north of Red Bluff Beach, a red-dirt track leads to an historical spot known as Wittacarra Creek, a popular beach fishing and boat launching site.

It was here that the murderous mutineers Wouter Loos and Jan Pelgrom de Bye were cast ashore to perish after their role in the 1629 massacre of 125 men, women and children – all survivors of the Batavia shipwreck on the Houtman Abrolhos Islands south of Kalbarri. Whether the pair survived their ordeal remains a mystery, but the spot has the dubious honour of being the first European settlement site on Australia's coast.

With a vista so wide it stretches all the way to the Zuytdorp Cliffs, Red Bluff's Pederick Lookout is a favourite whale watching and sunset spot, rolled into one. To reach the irresistible beach 700 metres below the rust-red cliffs, descend the rocky track to Red Bluff Beach for an invigorating swim. You can drive straight to the sand too, and on calm days go swimming, fishing and snorkel the rock pools. Return at day's end to watch the sun set Red Bluff on fire (not to be confused by Red Bluff at Quobba, further north).

Red Bluff Beach is close to town (just 15 minutes by bike), and the 500m-long trail to the lookout is wheelchair and pram-friendly.

01 Red Bluff Beach is quite the sight.
02 Snorkel or soak in the mini aquariums at Blue Holes. Don't forget your reef shoes!

JAKES POINT ³²/₁₀₀ ☐

Western Australia's #2 left-hand point break.

It's been a long time since this world-class wave was still a secret, but Jakes remains sacred to Kalbarri's local board riders. It's one of only three National Surfing Reserves on the West Australian coast, deemed a significant place in Australian Surf culture and history. Only Kalbarri's relative isolation keeps this iconic ride reasonably uncrowded, and that's just the way the locals like it.

'Jakes', the left-hand surf break at the southern end of Jacques Beach, is not for the faint-hearted. The wave breaks onto a shallow ledge, and low tides routinely expose the biting reef that snares wayward surfers. The only way to get out onto it is to jump off the rocks and paddle through the waves, which can be daunting for inexperienced surfers.

Although it's good even on smaller, waist-high days, it's the bigger, head-high to overhead swells that people wait for. Paddle onto the right wave, and it'll barrel for 200m down the line before spitting you out into the bay. Jakes is best surfed on a mid-tide with a south-westerly swell (the offshore winds are south-easterly). Nearly everyone gets washed over the rocks at some stage, so be prepared.

If you're a curious spectator, the best spot to watch the action is from the rock platform and cliffs at Jakes Point. Further down the wave, there's another break known as Little Jakes and a right-hander on the beach that are both more beginner-friendly.

SURF

It often seems like there's just one place to surf in Kalbarri, and that's Jakes – the wave that made this town famous.

In March 2010, local boardriders were central to this iconic surf spot being recognised as a National Surfing Reserve, declaring it off-limits to all kinds of commercialisation, even the town's boardrider club competitions. It's a cruel fate that such a swell-drenched section of coastline has so few good surfing spots and Kalbarri surfers are used to travelling as far south as Bowes River or north as Gnaraloo for good waves. These three breaks are well worth a play.

LUCKY BAY

BLUE HOLES

JAKES BEACH

Although the best swimming, snorkelling and windsurfing is inside the reef-protected lagoon at Lucky Bay campsite, if you chat with the caretaker and have a 4WD, he'll send you about 2km south down the beach to a left and right hand reef break that's the most consistent spot in the area. This is a wild stretch of coastline, though, so come prepared for anything.

Throughout winter, when long-period swells rock the coast, a clean left and right surf break forms off the back of the reef platform at the Blue Holes. It might still break onto a shallow ledge, but it's less intimidating than Jakes to the south. It works on southwest swells between waist-high and overhead conditions. Offshore winds are from the east to northeast.

If Jakes Point or Blue Holes are just too much or too crowded, Jakes Beach, just north of Jakes is an option, as is Back Beach, closer to town. Never as good as Kalbarri's halmark wave, both are fun for a bodysurf, bodyboard or just to get wet. Alternatively, further down the point from Jakes, a second section known as Little Jakes is also often worth riding.

RAINBOW JUNGLE ³³/₁₀₀ ☐

Get wild with soaring parrots and lose yourself in a labyrinth.

When your legs get weary and it's time for movies, mazes and dive-bombing birds, this place is Kalbarri's most dazzling attraction. Primarily, it's a parrot breeding centre with a raucous, free-flight, walk-in aviary that brings you face to face with the riotous calls and colour of some of the most brilliant parrots.

There are enormous blue and gold South American macaws and furry Eclectus parrots, black-headed caiques, and the largest flock of purple-crowned lorikeets in the world. You can feed the friendly ones and answer their pestering calls of 'hello', or escape the cacophony in the soothing tropical gardens, lily ponds and reflection pool.

While the birds provide the lion's share of entertainment, a 1400-square-metre maze thrills gamers who lose themselves within a labyrinth of hidden doors and deadends, brain teasers and towers. A notable highlight is the whale watching tower that peers over the Indian Ocean's 'Humpback Highway'.

Keeping the entertainment coming after dark, Parrotiso's Outdoor Cinema screens the latest movies every night at 7.30 pm, teamed with drinks and eats from its licensed pizza bar. Bring rugs and jackets to ward off the winter chill.

Rainbow Jungle is open daily from 9 am to 4 pm and provides wheelchair access to most of the park. Entry costs $16 for adults, $14 for concession card holders, $8 for kids and $40 for families. **rainbowjunglekalbarri.com**

KALBARRI ³⁴/₁₀₀ □
PELICAN FEEDING

Meet the town's feathery nomads.

Back in 1975, when a quirky doll museum called 'Fantasyland' studded Kalbarri's foreshore, owner Cliff Ross would wander across the road to the beach each morning and throw some fish to the pelicans. The story goes that the birds got very used to their daily feed, and if Cliff didn't turn up by 8.45 am, they would wander across to the museum to find him.

Today, a small team of volunteers continues the tradition, meeting the birds at 8.45 am each morning to feed them some fish and check on their health, removing fish hooks and line and providing first aid where needed. The birds nearly always turn up (unless the fishing is especially good at the mouth of the Murchison River), and the free feeding event has become so popular that it's officially a 'thing to do' in Kalbarri.

It's an excellent chance to get close to these nomadic Australian pelicans and learn cool things about them, like that they can stay airborne for up for 24 hours and soar at an altitude of 1000 metres or more. Sometimes the feeding sessions attract more pelicans than people, and other times (like when Lake Eyre fills up, luring them far inland), none might wander ashore for weeks. Donations are welcome, but dogs are not, and afterwards, you can head back across the road for breakfast at either the Pelican Café or nearby Black Rock Café.

MOUTH OF ³⁵/₁₀₀ ☐
THE MURCH

01

Paddle the mighty Murchison, the second-longest in the west.

From the distant Robinson Ranges, the Murchison River colours the landscape for 820km, carving a deep, rugged path through crumbling sandstone before calming at last on the edge of the sea. It's a diverse and magnificent river to paddle, providing access for canoeing adventures all the way from the Murchison River gorge downstream to where a protective sandbar holds back the sea.

Bring any boat you can to get exploring – a SUP, kayak, canoe or tinny – plus pool toys for the kids, a picnic basket and stacks of sunscreen. You can hire all kinds of boats from Kalbarri Boat Hire or take your own tinny fishing for arm-

02

aching catches of mulloway, yellowfin whiting and black bream.

Interestingly, the first European to discover the mighty Murchison River did so only by chance. While searching WA for a river fabled to be one of the longest in the world, daring explorer Sir George Grey was twice shipwrecked, stranded, nearly drowned, speared in the hip and finally, lost on the Kalbarri coastline.

He found the mouth of the Murchison River but then had to walk all the way to Perth, surviving by drinking liquid mud and with considerable help from a Noongar man called Kaiber. The upside for Grey was that he learnt to speak the Noongar language, and his subsequent passion for Indigenous people made him Captain and Resident Magistrate in WA's original settlement at King George Sound, Albany.

On a coast well known for its treacherous seas and surf, the mouth of the Murchison River provides

something of an oasis. On hot days, locals and travellers float all kinds of boats in this protected pool, and upstream, stake out sandy river beaches to picnic beneath the eucalypts and dare each other onto rope swings.

You can organise your own adventures or join a full or half-day paddling trip on the river's lower reaches with Kalbarri Boat Hire, who provide all gear, food and transfers (find them on the foreshore on Grey Street). Far upstream inside Kalbarri National Park, Kalbarri Adventure Tours runs more adventurous expeditions that lead you deep into the river gorge for hiking, paddling and waterfall play. Tours with both of these companies are suitable for kids and range from $60-70 for kids and $90 for adults.

01 The 820km Murchison River empties into the ocean at Kalbarri.
02 Kalbarri Boat Hire offer half day canoe safaris, dropping you 15km upriver via 4wd.

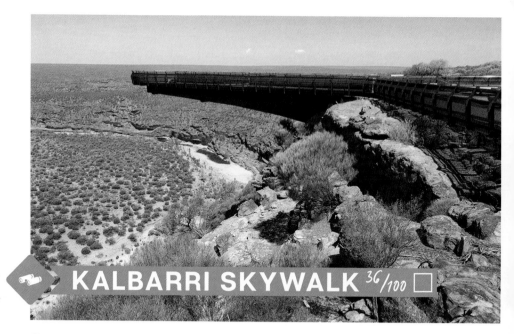

KALBARRI SKYWALK ³⁶/₁₀₀ ☐

Step out over this abyss for dizzying, downward views.

Adventuring far inland, a rugged abyss pulls you to its rocky edge, to teeter 100 metres above the vast, vibrant wilderness of Murchison Gorge. The biggest attraction here is the newest: a masterful pair of cantilevered platforms hanging you high out over the gorge for dizzying views beneath your feet.

Known by its Nanda name kaju yatka, meaning 'sky' and 'to walk', the twin Skywalk lookouts extend 25 and 17 metres over the gorge at the Inyaka Wookai Watju site. Providing universal access to woo every visitor, the Skywalk is the centrepiece of a $24 million makeover revealed in June 2020 that includes a power-neutral kiosk

and extensive interpretive signage to take visitors on a Dreamtime journey, following the snaking path of Beemarra serpent, sandblasted into the walkway.

The Skywalk provides a breathtaking introduction to this remarkable gorge, carved for 80km through soft, colourful layers of tumblagooda sandstone. Although it's not as phyiscally demanding as other attractions in the park, here you'll learn the most about it.

Kalbarri National Park opens from sunrise to sunset (although there are no gates anywhere) and charges a $15 vehicle entry fee. Get an early start to your day's exploring to avoid the wintertime crowds and summer's intense heat, but linger here until late to watch the setting sun ignite the Murchison's stunning, golden gorge.

NATURE'S WINDOW 37/100 ☐

See the Murchison river canyon through this iconic spyhole.

This iconic rock window frames a startling scene of the Murchison's vibrant canyon and the winding river at its feet. Providing a macro snapshot of an expansive vista, Nature's Window sharpens your focus on the intricate bands of bright red, yellow and white tumblagooda sandstone and the distant waterway sculpting these cliffs.

In the cooler hours, the 400m-long stroll to Nature's Window doesn't take long, but footprints along the track provide plenty of distractions. As you wander, scan the rippled rock at your feet for some perfectly cast scurry prints of long-extinct arthropods, now fossilised into the red rock.

For views that are just your own, leave the happy snappers at Nature's Window and walk about 300m down the track to your own shaded cave spot. This is a perfect place to sit and sip, nibble your snacks and stare out over the Murchison River. Plenty of people hang around here for sunset, but if you can make it for sunrise, you'll get to soak up the scene in solitude.

All roads through Kalbarri National park are sealed and suitable for 2WD vehicles, however in some spots, including Nature's Window, you'll have to unhitch your trailer or caravan before entering. Explorers should pack plenty of drinking water, plus sunscreen, snacks, sturdy footwear and a hat. The kiosk at the Skywalk can refuel you with coffee, cold drinks and carbs.

THE LOOP TRAIL $^{38}/_{100}$ ☐

Find out what's through the sandstone window.

If you want to do more than gaze over the Murchison River gorge, you'll love the Loop Walk. Covering 9km, this class 4 hike beyond Nature's Window, continues over the Eurypterid trace fossils – evidence of some of the earliest terrestrial life forms.

Scramble down into the gorge to a sandy beach at the water's edge, and sit beneath the river gums to watch sea eagles soaring on thermals before rock-hopping downstream. There are plenty of markers, but no real 'trail' inside the gorge, and the river's water level will determine the route you take. You'll get plenty of chances to cool off, too.

Despite its harsh outward appearance, the gorge hosts an abundance of life.

Emus might be seen walking the trails, ignoring the photo ops, and during wildflower season, the riverside verge explodes with colour.

When it finally leaves the water's edge, the trail climbs steadily back onto the gorge rim via a rocky staircase of boulders and slabs. After the stiff climb, you get to admire views through Nature's Window one more time while you catch your breath.

To get the most from this three to four hour-long adventure, set out in the early morning and carry plenty of water. There isn't much shade and it can be 10°C hotter than on the rim. Over summer, temperatures can flare to as much as 50°C, so you must start the Loop Trail before 7 am (when access closes). There are stories of hikers' shoes melting on the rocks, and the flies can be a menace!

THE RIVER TRAILS ³⁹/₁₀₀ ☐

Hike beyond the barricades on the Murchison's river trails.

Cool wintertime rains unleash riotous wildflower blooms in Kalbarri National Park, colouring the vast sand plains and peppering the road to Hawks Head and Ross Graham lookout. Far from the madding crowds on a remote bend in the river gorge, Ross Graham lookout remembers the Kalbarri conservationist who died tragically, aged 31, with a dramatic river vista and walk trail.

This 700-metre track provides the quickest route into the upper Murchison, where you can swim or paddle the day away. Nearby, Hawks Head lookout is a great picnic area.

Further downstream, the fun River Trail at Z Bend provides an intense, scenic scramble to some tranquil waterholes

in the gorge. This 2.6km return track (class 4) starts easy, following the same well-worn path you follow to reach the Z Bend Lookout.

At the well-signed fork, detour to the lookout, then continue your descent to the river: climbing over rocks, through rock chutes and down ladders to get up close and personal with the park's highest cliffs. This two hour-return track is not for the faint-hearted, but school-age kids shouldn't have much trouble.

As you explore, keep an eye out for black-flanked rock wallabies, a species considered long extinct before rock climbers sighted some in 2015. That kick-started a wallaby relocation program to bolster the park's population. When you go, set out early on the trail to avoid heat, carry plenty of water and snacks, and wear decent shoes.

SHARK BAY

Located as far west as you can get on Australia's mainland, the seaside town of Denham is so remote it has to make its own drinking water. But it's what surrounds the town that pulls a crowd: overlapping marine and coastal sanctuaries that are 2.2 million hectares large and teeming with life.

Shark Bay's opalescent seas safeguard the world's largest seagrass banks and the diverse marine creatures that feed on them, rolling across coral reefs and cockle shell beaches and filling a bay so salty that only rare, ancient stromatolites manage to grow. Up to 6000 loggerhead and green sea turtles call this wild underwater world home, along with 10 per cent of the world's dugongs and Monkey Mia's famous dolphins too.

Meeting all four natural criteria for world heritage listing, Shark Bay ticks a lot of boxes, and visitors can choose to explore in an impossible number of ways. Launch a boat, paddle a sea kayak, join a sunset sailing cruise or go snorkelling.

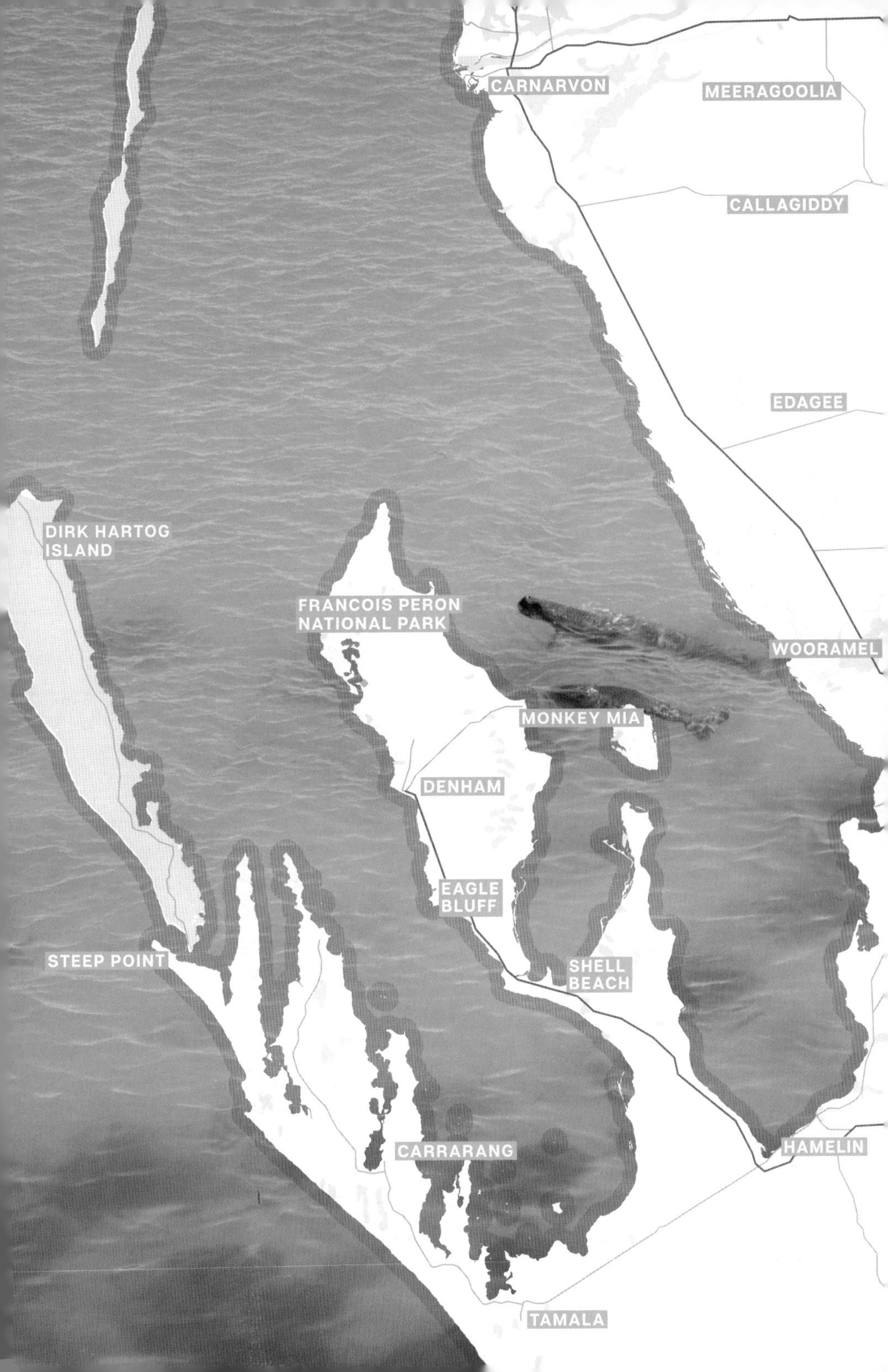

CARNARVON

MEERAGOOLIA

CALLAGIDDY

EDAGEE

DIRK HARTOG ISLAND

FRANCOIS PERON NATIONAL PARK

WOORAMEL

MONKEY MIA

DENHAM

STEEP POINT

EAGLE BLUFF

SHELL BEACH

CARRARANG

HAMELIN

TAMALA

Western Australia rolling out the red carpet on the drive into Francois Peron National Park.

There are clifftop hikes and pearling relics to discover, a deeply relaxing (albeit scalding) artesian hot tub to bathe in, and lots of sandy-footed solitude awaits campers in Francois Peron National Park.

Anglers venture to this faraway fishing ground chasing big pelagics and even bigger stories, and to stand above the 200km-long, end-of-world scarps at Zuytdorp Cliffs that plunge 250 metres into a treacherous, pounding and rebounding sea. These are the legendary cliffs that terrified and shipwrecked the earliest Dutch, French and British sailors. It's conceivable that the Malgana, Nanda and Yingkarta peoples met some of them after they stumbled ashore, and long before that, told stories about this landscape before it cracked along a fault line during an epic earthquake 10,000 years ago.

Across this region, a solitary town pulls travellers out of the wilds. Denham exudes a warm, outback-meets-the-sea charm and provides everything you really need. Use it as a base for jaunts into Francois Peron National Park, Monkey Mia (for wild dolphin feeding) or to resupply after adventures on remote Dirk Hartog Island. Denham provides all kinds of accommodation choices, and you'll find historical and unique places to stay on its fringes too.

Just waiting for self-sufficient travellers, the wilds of the Peron and Edel Land Peninsulas are where you'll touch the last of the day's rays, camp on truly deserted beaches and adventure onto sandy red tracks that take you far, far away.

STAY

Whether you like to rough it under the stars along rarely visited beaches or lap it up in luxury and at pool-side bars, Shark Bay is for you.

For those that are self-contained and self-sufficient, there's an almost endless array of absolute beachfront camping on offer. Primarily managed by Parks and Wildlife, it's usually cheap, often has clean, but basic, facilities and the views, fishing and relaxing are to die for. If proper beds, chilled cocktails and wildlife-free swims are more your thing, you can indulge in comfort at Monkey Mia or a few places in Dehnham itself. The choice is yours.

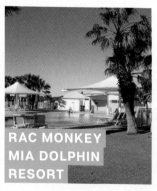

RAC MONKEY MIA DOLPHIN RESORT

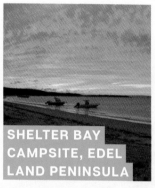

SHELTER BAY CAMPSITE, EDEL LAND PENINSULA

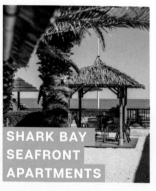

SHARK BAY SEAFRONT APARTMENTS

On the sheltered, western shores of Peron Peninsula, overlooking the dolphin feeding beach, RAC Monkey Mia is an unexpected oasis of luxury in this otherwise barren landscape. Arrive in a rig with your own beds on board, or stay in luxury eco-cabins, swim in the resort pool and catch sunset from the Monkey Bar with something cold in your hand.
parksandresorts.rac. com.au/monkey-mia

We could have highlighted any of Shark Bay's fantastic national park campsites – they're all great. But Shelter Bay is affordable and ideally located for adventures around Steep Point or before trips to Dirk Hartog Island. There are basic facilities, you can launch a boat from the beach, and the best fishing spots are close by (adults $11, concession $7 and kids $3). Book ahead at
parks.dpaw.wa.gov.au/ park-stay

Overlooking Denham Sound and snug in the centre of town, Seafront Apartments are waterfront, self-contained and comfortable, and the central courtyard is a friendly hub where travellers can meet, compare notes and share adventures. A range of one and two-bedroom apartments come with air-con and ensuites, essential to escape the summer-time heat.
sharkbayseafrontapart- ments.com.au

STEEP POINT ⁴⁰/₁₀₀ ☐

01

Journey to the edge of the world (with your fishing gear).

North, south, east and west: it's a significant achievement to stand on the four most extreme compass points on the Australian mainland, and with a visit to Steep Point, you can tick off the most western vista and stand on the most remote, least visited and most aptly named extreme point on the continent.

It demands a seriously committed 4WD journey: the track is rocky, rough and (let's be real) largely uncomfortable, and the weather is undeniably extreme. Time your trip for March to August to avoid big summertime surf and wild winds, and before you hit the track, deflate your tyres to at least 20psi to save them (and your fillings) from undue damage. Most of all, pack your fishing rods.

Steep Point studs the top of the Edel Land Peninsula at the end of the ruler-edged, 200km-long Zuytdorp Cliffs (pronounced zowt-dorp). These cliffs tower 250 metres above a raging, tempestuous sea and were formed around 10,000 years ago when an earthquake shattered the land along this fault line. Ever since, the cliffs have been relentlessly battered by wind, waves and even mega-tsunamis believed responsible for throwing giant, 700-ton boulders onto the cliffs at Dirk Hartog Island.

Named after a Dutch merchant shipwrecked against the cliffs in 1712, Zuytdorp's steep limestone walls plunge directly into deep water where giant pelagic fish feed close to shore. Standing atop the cliffs and rocks, anglers commonly reel in big tuna, Spanish mackerel and thumping spangled emperor, and no shortage of sharks too.

The main spot to fish is called The Oven, a low point in the cliffs just east of Steep Point. It's so good that keen anglers drive all day just to spend a weekend fishing

here, but success depends on having the right gear. You'll need to balloon your bait out off the rocks and get a four-pronged gaff on a rope to retrieve your fish and haul it six to 12 metres back up the cliff. If you're bringing a boat, you can launch it from Shelter Bay, but remember there's a marine sanctuary until you're clear of Surf Point.

The remote, bush camps at Shelter Bay, The Oven and False Entrance offer only the barest of facilities (drop toilets at the Oven and Shelter Bay, none at False Entrance), but that doesn't seem to dent their popularity. Book ahead during the peak winter months and on weekends. Campsites cost $11 per adult (per night), $7 for concession cardholders and $3 for kids (parks.dpaw.wa.gov.au/park-stay).

01 The Zuytdorp Cliffs stretch 200km between Steep Point and Kalbarri.

02 A spearfisherman with his prized catch, a 15kg Spanish mackerel.

03 Deflate your tyres for the long, rough drive into Steep Point.

 # DIRK HARTOG ⁴¹/₁₀₀ ☐
ISLAND

Let the angling adventure begin.

From the highest point on the WA coastline, near the first patch of Australia ever set foot upon by a European, you can be the last person in the country to watch the sun go down. Prepare to tick some boxes on Dirk Hartog Island and reel in crazy-big catches of fish, ogle sky-high blowholes and go snorkelling, turtle spotting and whale watching too.

It's not uncommon for anglers to reel in 25kg Spanish mackerel or giant trevally off the rocks or catch crayfish bigger than your arm. You can see loggerhead turtles hatching in April at Turtle Beach, and the sanctuary at Surf Point nurtures a nursery of sharks, best observed chasing fish through the shallows from July to October. Dirk Hartog is a pristine and difficult to reach destination, and, with visitor numbers limited to just 20 vehicles at a time, you'll truly feel like you've arrived at the edge of the world.

WA's European backstory began on the island in 1616 when Dutchman Dirk Hartog nailed an inscribed pewter plate onto a timber plank and mounted it on the hilltop at Cape Inscription. Today, the Hartog Plate resides in Amsterdam's Rijksmuseum, but a replica in its place and interpretive panels deliver the full history lesson for visitors.

Difficult (and pricey) access to the island holds back the masses. First, you must

01 With visitors to the island limited to 20 cars at a time, you can enjoy a beach to yourself!

tackle the 220km-long 4WD journey along the Edel Land Peninsula to Shelter Beach near Steep Point, then board the barge to the island, forking out more than you've ever paid before for a 15-minute boat trip. Over the peak winter months, return barge transfers cost from $510 per vehicle, with extra fees charged for passengers, trailers and national park camping fees. It costs less to travel on the weekends, but you'll need to book months in advance to secure a spot.

On the island, there are nine national park campgrounds to choose from, all costing $20 per person, per night, plus $3 for kids. Select one of the west coast camps for cliff-based fishing and stellar sunsets, or base yourself on the sheltered eastern shores for snorkelling, flatwater paddling and kid-play.

It might be bucket-list, but this adventure guarantees seclusion, and you'll share your island fling with no more than 20 other vehicles at a time. The unbelievable fishing will save you a fortune in seafood dinners and is best from May to July. When you go, take extreme care when casting off the island's remote coastal cliffs and beaches, and when the waves get too dicey, drive to the island's south-west corner to watch the blowholes instead. These boom when the swell builds to more than 2.5 metres, exploding through blowholes with a force that makes their jet sprays visible 20km away.

Exploring inland, be sure to check out the island's lolly-pink Rose Lake. Its name celebrates Rose de Freycinet, who stowed away on her explorer husband's ship (of Freycinet National Park fame) and, in doing so, became the first women to circumnavigate the globe. Rose Lake gets its spectacular hue from the same bacteria that turn Hutt Lagoon rosy, and looks impressive almost all year round.

Providing refuge to the west's rarest and near-extinct marsupial species, Dirk Hartog Island today harbours rufous and banded hare wallabies, dibblers and Shark Bay bandicoots, reintroduced as part of WA's Return to 1616 recovery program. These nocturnal critters are why driving at night is a no-no, but you just might catch one in your spotlight wandering after dark.

Camping on Dirk Hartog Island is permitted year-round, but the time you'll want to visit is over the cool winter months when the barge runs (March to mid-December), temperatures are bearable, and humpback whales and whale sharks pass on by.

It might seem like a remote and rough campers' destination, but the island's Eco Lodge lets you sleep sand-free with ensuite beachfront rooms, gourmet meals, beach toys and a bar. The resort also has beachfront camps that are a cut above the national park sites and come with hot showers, toilets and a camp kitchen. Find out more at dirkhartogisland.com.

02 Be the last person in the country to watch the sun go down.

02

HAMELIN POOL ⁴²/₁₀₀ ☐

Discover what it takes to survive 2000 years in a hypersaline sea.

Scientists get very excited about stromatolites, but author Bill Bryson probably described them best in his book Down Under as: lustreless, grey and very much like large cow-pats. Yet as living examples of the earliest life on earth, stromatolites have proven that looks ain't everything when it comes to survival, and Hamelin Pool is one of only two places in the world where these prehistoric beauties grow.

They thrive in water so salty at Shark Bay, it precludes the survival of all other marine life. In fact, stromatolites have dominated life on earth for 80 per cent of its long history, quietly generating the oxygen needed for everything else to flourish. Hamelin Pool's hypersalinity means these 2000-year-old stromatolites have no predator, apart from the careless humans who

leave the boardwalk that protects this rare colony. You'll find them at Hamelin Pool, 27km off the North West Coastal Highway, where a boardwalk elevates you above the stromatolites, and interpretive signs quell your curiosity.

You can overnight at Hamelin Station Stay or drive on to Hamelin Pool Caravan Park, where you can tackle the Boolagoorda Walk (1.4km), looping past the remains of a pioneer-era telegraph station and an old quarry where coquina – tightly compressed blocks of natural Hamelin cockles – were quarried to build Denham's earliest buildings. These include the Old Pearler Restaurant and the Shark Bay Shellblock Church (St Andrew by the Sea). More interesting but less well known are the ancient Indigenous wells, dug into the coquina along the shoreline north of the telegraph station that

appear as circular depressions in the otherwise flat rock.

Owned by Bush Heritage Australia, Hamelin Station is a 202,000-hectare former sheep station, now sanctuary where you can camp or spend a night in historical shearers quarters (from $80, hamelinstationstay.com.au). Close to the stromatolites, Hamelin Pool Caravan Park has campsites from $11 per person, and its Telegraph Station Museum (tours daily) conserves a slice of the west's early communication history and has an excellent presentation on the stromatolites, including a living one in its aquarium (hamelinpoolcaravanpark.com).

01 Get up close with the world's oldest living fossils.

02 Interpretive signs and a timber boardwalk guide you through the stromatolites.

01

Swim off a beach made entirely of cockle shells.

As you crunch your way to the water's edge at Shell Beach, you might wonder where all the sand is, but Shell Beach is just that: a 60km-long stretch of tiny Shark Bay cockle shells (Fragum erugatum), deposited up to 10 metres deep. Billions of shells create undulating white dunes that date back 4000 years, lapped by an exquisite turquoise bay that stretches endlessly to the far horizon.

Few water views are as lovely as this one, and in this bright blue bay, you'll feel deliciously warm and remarkably buoyant! That's because this shallow scoop of water is super saline, thanks to a sand bar across the northern boundaries of Hamelin Pool and L'Haridon Bight that holds back the swell that might otherwise wash in and replenish the bay.

Free of predators and nurtured by a photosynthetic organism called zooxanthellae, WA's own cockle lives long and dies naturally, washing up on the shoreline in the billions. The entire beach at the southern end of the bight is made up of the shells which extend far out into the bay.

Walking barefoot on the shells is a dicey business (reef shoes help), but the biggest challenge you'll face is when you attempt to build a cockle shell castle. Bring a snorkel, and you might eyeball an olive-headed sea snake, foraging for food. You'll find Shell Beach Conservation Park signposted about 85km west of the Overlander Highway turn-off on the road to Denham.

EAT

What Shark Bay's food scene lacks in delicacy, it more than makes up for in heartiness and ol' fashioned service.

There's a suprising range of good eateries around Denham. Choose from poolside bars (RAC Monkey Mia) or eat above a shark feeding tank (Ocean Park Aquarium), or even in buildings of shell. Everywhere has exceptional veiws over the water, too. These three are the highlights.

WESTERN WOODFIRED PIZZA

THE OLD PEARLER

SHARK BAY HOTEL

Especially in the most remote locations, good woodfired pizza is a rare delight. Takeaway only, Western Woodfired Pizza gathers locals and travellers alike, who order then enjoy the meal watching the sun set over the sound, chilled drinks in hand. Along with the popular favourites, gluten free, vegetarian and vegan options are available. Drop in to order. sharkbaypizza.com.au

With an intriguing heritage and a fresh-from-the-sea menu, the Old Pearler is one of the best places to eat in Shark Bay. It's built entirely from rough-cut coquina (cockle shell) bricks cut from the Hamelin Bay quarry in 1974, making it worth visiting just for its looks alone. The locally-inspired Aussie menu and friendly service explain why you'll need a booking.
Call 08 9948 1373.

Long-time locals call it the Old Pub, and if you can snag a bench on the balcony at happy hour, there's no better place on earth to enjoy a cold drink. The hotel overlooks the esplanade and catches the afternoon sea breeze. The traditional menu is pub-like and simple, but the servings are deliciously large and the atmosphere, always friendly. sharkbayhotelwa.com.au

SHARK BAY'S 44/100 □
WILD COASTAL CAMPS

01

Spend a wild night at Shark Bay's most accessible coastal camps.

On the Peron Peninsula's western flank, the coastline rises and falls over captivating bluffs and blissfully deserted beaches. Rustic, no-frills campsites dot the shoreline, tempting travellers off the road into Denham to spend a solitary night at one of four turquoise bays.

Goulet Bluff, Whalebone Beach, Fowlers Camp and Eagle Bluff are all different names for the same thing: perfect, sheltered places to fish and swim, launch a boat or beachcomb, climb lofty headlands and wander along a boardwalk. Choose carefully because

this camping opportunity is for one night only, and you'll need to book and pay on the day you intend to stay as numbers are restricted to just four groups per camp.

Choose Goulet Bluff for access to Shell Beach, Whalebone Bay for its flat, caravan-friendly sites, Fowlers for beach fishing and protection from the wind, and Eagle Bluff to snorkel and watch the ospreys and sea eagles overhead.

Eagle Bluff is just 20 minutes out of Denham, so even if you're not camping here, it's worth visiting just to stroll the 400m boardwalk that loops along the high cliffs and elevates you above rocky isles offshore and the dugongs that groom the seagrass below (bring binoculars). It was here that Captain H.M. Denham etched his name on a rock when he stepped ashore in 1858. That rock is now on display in Denham's Pioneer Park, but Eagle Bluff remains a top sunset picnic spot.

Whalebone Bay is another favourite, shallow blue bay that acts as something of a nursery for Shark Bay's namesake species. Climb the hill to the south or paddle silently by on your kayak or SUP to spot the juvenile sharks. There's plenty of wildlife along this seemingly barren coastline, and it's not just the whiting, snapper, bream and kingfish that might tempt you to launch a tinny.

Starfish and cockles stud the shallows, emus scavenge the bush, and you might even spot euro kangaroos digging in the sand above the high

tide mark for the potable water found just below the surface. It's a technique copied by Indigenous peoples for thousands of years, and you can try it yourself!

Signposted off Shark Bay Road between 36km and 18km south of Denham, the four camping areas cost $15 per night and provide no facilities. Dogs are permitted, but campfires are not, and graded roads permit 2WD access year-round. You must bring your own drinking water (or buy it from Denham's desalination depot) and take away all rubbish too. To book your site, phone the Shark Bay Discovery Visitor Centre on (08) 9948 1590.

01 Kaleidescopic coastines in Francois Peron National Park.

02 You can camp for 24 hours at Whalebone Bay, just 27km south of Denham.

OCEAN PARK AQUARIUM

⁴⁵/100 ☐

Watch sharks feeding while you dine.

You never knew you wanted to get this close to a feeding shark, but at Ocean Park, standing an arm's length away from lemon sharks and sandbar whalers fighting over a fish head is a curiously captivating experience. There's plenty of Shark Bay marine life on show at this outback aquarium, including stingrays, sea snakes and rescued sea turtles, and while it might not rate against big-city aquariums, in many ways, Ocean Park offers more.

Head here for entertaining tours, guided by marine scientists who know Shark Bay's marine life well and can answer all your questions. Ocean Park began as an aquaculture farm for pink snapper, but today its focus has shifted to research and conservation.

You can dive with sharks in the aquarium's shark lagoon or watch them feed from the safety of Ocean restaurant, overlooking the large outdoor pools where shark feeding sessions take place six times daily. Powered by one of the largest solar installations in the west, the aquarium is impressively eco-sensitive as a rehabilitation centre for Shark Bay's marine creatures.

If you love to dive or want to learn, Ocean Park runs the only PADI dive courses and tours in Shark Bay, including to Steep Point on the very western edge of the country. During the peak winter months (April to October), aquarium tours run from 9 am to 3.30 pm. Entry costs $27 for adults, $24 for concession cardholders and $19 for kids (aged 4-16, free for under fours). oceanpark.com.au

PERON 46/100 ☐
HOT TUB

Take a scorching dunk in this pioneer-era pool.

Overflowing with 44-degree artesian bore water on the edge of Francois Peron National Park, this deeply relaxing hot tub soothes weary bones after a day of corrugated, off-road action. The water is scalding so you'll feel like a frog in a hot pot as you dare your toes in deeper and deeper until you're soaking up to your neck in the mineral-rich pool.

There's no way around it, this is one hot pond, but if you team your hot dunk with an exhilarating, icy shower afterwards, it's the quintessential, conversation-starting ending to any visit to Francois Peron National Park.

You'll find the hot tub at the old Peron Homestead, a former sheep station and heritage precinct where you can take an historical wander along the Pepper Trail through old stockyards, a shearing shed and the shearers quarters (45 minutes return). An interpretive centre showcases the devastating impact that pastoralism had on the Peron Peninsula's fragile ecosystem, entirely wiping out rare, endangered marsupials like woylies, banded and rufous hare-wallabies and quendas.

Despite constructing a barrier fence across the peninsula to keep out feral animals and decades of breeding and release attempts, only two reintroduced species are thriving – malleefowls and nocturnal greater bilbies.

The Peron Heritage Precinct provides a grassy picnic area, barbecues, toilets and showers, is free to enter, and is accessible via sealed roads off the road that links Denham and Monkey Mia.

BIG LAGOON, 47/100 ☐
FRANCOIS PERON
NATIONAL PARK

01

Stay and play on Shark Bay's biggest tidal inlet.

In Francois Peron's red sand wilderness, Big Lagoon is a gin-clear standout, with waterfront camping, flatwater paddling and angling so good you'll feel like you're cheating. Grooming the seagrass beds, dugongs and sea turtles commune in some of the clearest water on earth, and beyond this bay that the Malgana people call thalganjangu, lofty red dunes roll along a tricoloured coastline, studded with pearling relics and shell middens for intrepid explorers to find.

Launch a boat to fish, encounter dolphins hunting at the sea entrance, or paddle a kayak 20 minutes across the lagoon to lay your footprints on deserted shores and scale the steep dunes that separate Big Lagoon from the sea. The largest tidal inlet in Shark Bay World Heritage Area, Big Lagoon is a flooded version of what the Malgana call a birrida (a large, circular clay pan), now linked to the sea to create a shallow water sanctuary and an important nursery for fish, rays and crustaceans.

Beyond Big Lagoon, a slow, sandy 4WD track continues 50km north to the tip of Cape Peron and four beachfront camps at Gregories, South Gregories, Bottle Bay and Herald Bight. It's all off-road and corrugated, so you'll have to deflate

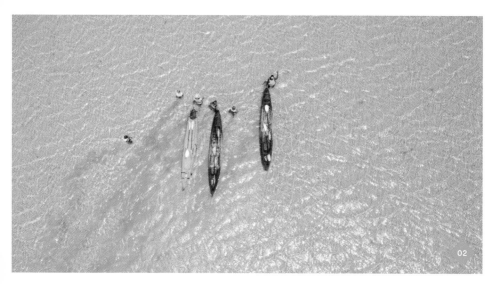

02

your tyres, but there's plenty of history to unearth en route.

Pull off at Kraskoe's Tank, the corrugated-iron home of legendary Leon Krasker who, with one cork leg and a horse named Battler, once rode a 70km-long return journey from Denham to Herald Bight each week to buy pearls and collect the pearlers' mail. But a spooked horse, a bad fall and a broken good leg, back in September 1916, were to be the end of 39-year-old Krasker, who attempted to drag himself back to his tank shelter and died en route.

Continuing north, the track smoothes out alongside a series of shallow birridas, their shimmering shorelines littered with pelican feathers and reflecting every cloudy sky. Turn off to Cattle Well to catch a feed of whiting and watch cormorants drying their wings in the breeze, before pushing on to explore Cape Peron.

Of the national park's five waterfront camps, Big Lagoon is the most interesting and the easiest to access, just 12km along the track. There's an excellent camp shelter with free gas BBQs and picnic tables, plus toilets and a basic boat ramp. Fees are $11 per adult, $7 for concession cardholders and $3 for kids, payable by self-registration at the national park entrance.

Outside the national park and just 3.4km along the sealed Denham-Monkey Mia Road, Little Lagoon is a calm, miniature birrida where you can swim and picnic, SUP and kitesurf, and sample a taste of the national park wilds without having to deflate your tyres.

01 Join Wula Gura Nyinda for a full-day kayak and cultural adventure.

02 Flatwater paddling and gin-clear water will entice you out into the lagoon.

GREGORIES BEACH, *48/100* □
FRANCOIS PERON
NATIONAL PARK

Snorkel a coral lagoon and discover shell middens atop towering dunes.

The iconic, red Peron sandstone plunges into the sea, colouring this rosy beach where travellers gather at sunset, cradling chilly beers and fishing rods, their toes dug into the sand. A beautiful, shallow lagoon hugs the shore, and the coral-fringed wall that holds back the sea calls snorkellers to kick out across the bay, spotting juvenile reef sharks, rays and the occasional sea snake.

Afterwards, you can warm up on the fiery-red sand dunes that rise to great heights at the southern end of the beach, peppered with pioneer-era pearling relics and half-buried shell middens. Breathtaking Indian Ocean sunsets burn brightly here, igniting scenes that photographers will cherish forever. Glowing at sunset and when the moon is full, the dunes create unforgettable vistas, beckoning walkers to add their footprints to a nocturnal maze of tiny animal tracks and linger for ghostly scenes atop the dunes.

There's an undeniable, wild beauty in this secluded spot, so before you tackle the sandy track all the way to Gregories, pack snorkelling gear and enough supplies and drinking water to see you through a couple of glorious nights.

Here, and at South Gregories too, large, mostly private campsites face the beach. Each have their own tracks down onto the sand so in a few quick steps you can be floating or fishing for a catch of whiting, flathead, mackerel or snapper.

Gregories beats South Gregories for facilities – toilets, picnic tables and free gas barbecues – but if you have a tinny to launch, head to Bottle Bay for 4WD access to the beach and bathe in the cosy nook nestled inside the point reserved just for swimming. You can fish, camp and paddle here too, and from Bottle Bay, the clifftop trail at Cape Peron is just 6km away.

The track gets noticeably rougher and softer as you drive deeper into Francois Peron National Park, so reduce your tyre pressure to at least 20psi before setting out, and again when the midday heat spikes the sand temperature if you need to. There's a compressor at the park entrance to inflate them when you exit. As you explore, remember to stick to the tracks, keep off the birridas, and slow down to give way to the euro kangaroos, echidnas and thorny devils that call this place home.

01 Explore the red sand dunes at the southern end of the beach.

02 Keep an eye out for native animals including echidnas and thorny devils.

CAPE PERON, ⁴⁹/₁₀₀ □
FRANCOIS PERON
NATIONAL PARK

Watch Shark Bay's marine life on the hunt from this lofty clifftop trail.

At the very tip of the Peron Peninsula, vast, restless flocks of cormorants, gulls and terns stake out the sand, squawking and studding a colourful scene between burnt red cliffs and the turquoise sea. High above, the Wanamalu Trail teeters on the edge of 250,000-year-old Peron sandstone cliffs, elevating walkers over the translucent shoreline where eagle rays, green turtles and shovel-nosed sharks shoot through the shallows on the hunt.

Only from this lofty trail can you really fathom the sheer size of Shark Bay's mammoth world heritage area: 2.2 million hectares teeming with loggerhead turtles, 10 per cent of the world's dugongs, dolphins, and not surprisingly for a place called 'Shark Bay', plenty of sharks too.

But the best thing you'll ever see at Cape Peron is a rare show indeed and

The Wanamalu Trail follows the clifftop between twin lookouts at Cape Peron and Skipjack Point (90mins, 3km return). Visit in wildflower season when the dunes blaze with colour, transformed by the blue flowering Dampiera incana and Shark Bay daises, white myrtles, yellow wattles and wild tomato bushes.

a genuinely wild contrast to the touristy spectacle of dolphin feeding at Monkey Mia. Here, female bottlenose dolphins famously round up sea mullet in the shallows, herding the fish onto the sand and hydroplaning dangerously in less than a foot of water to trap and capture their feed. If you do get to see it, it'll rate as one of the most incredible things you witness on this coast. If not, check out National Geographic's Dolphins, The Wild Side for some old, but still epic, footage of Shark Bay's dolphin girls in action.

This track is best walked in the early morning when the marine creatures and birds are more active. If you are day tripping through the national park, the 50km-long 4WD trip to the tip of Cape Peron takes around 90 minutes, giving you plenty of time to explore this and other beaches, and go fishing, paddling and snorkelling.

01 Red sands create a striking contrast against turquoise sea.

02 Follow the 3km Wanamalu Trail for gorgeous vistas and wildlife spotting.

01

The world-famous wild dolphins are just the beginning.

It's to encounter some of the world's most famous wild dolphins that travellers seek out this idyllic blue cove. But what will tether you here is one seriously beautiful beach, a sprawling beachfront resort with great facilities and a baffling number of ways to have fun on the sea.

For over 50 years, a special affinity has been fostered between bottlenose dolphins and humans. Back in the 1960s, a local fisherman began sharing some of his daily catch with the dolphins, and almost every morning since, a small pod of wild female bottlenose dolphins has shown up at Monkey Mia's Dolphin Beach for a free feed of fish.

The feeding sessions are strictly controlled to ensure the dolphins remain hungry enough to forage in the wild and continue feeding their nursing offspring. Only five female adults get fed regularly,

although you'll often get close to their offspring, too, while standing ankle-deep on the shoreline at Dolphin Beach.

To join the fun, head to the Monkey Mia Visitor Centre at 7.45 am on any morning for a quick briefing before park rangers lead you down to the beach. The dolphins are fed up to three times, so if the first session is too crowded, you can come back later in the day or watch the action from the nearby jetty.

The Visitor Centre has excellent interpretive displays and collects the national park's daily entrance fees: adults $15, concession $10, kids $5, and families $35. If you stay a few days, monthly passes are good value (adults $25, concession $20, child $12, and families $60).

With tourists lined up along the water's edge, the experience might be dubiously 'wild', but few would deny that seeing Monkey Mia's dolphins up close is thrilling. If you want to avoid the touristy feeding spectacle, hire a kayak or SUP and paddle the lagoon instead. There's a very good chance dolphins will swim close by anyway, along with dugongs and sea turtles too.

There's plenty to do at Monkey Mia, from catamaran cruises, to Indigenous cultural tours or even learning to kitesurf, but it costs nothing to enjoy the good fishing, snorkelling and swimming. If you love to walk, the Wulyibidi Yaninyina Trail crosses the coastal dunes to an Indigenous shelter cave, an historical gravesite, and a bird hide where you might spot zebra finches, variegated fairy-wrens, osprey and emus (4km/1.5 hours).

No one really remembers how Monkey Mia got its name, but some say it comes from the Indigenous word Mia, meaning refuge or resting place, and remembers a pearling lugger called Monkey which found safe anchorage here in the late 19th century, Monkey's refuge.

Located 24km from Denham, Monkey Mia Dolphin Resort provides all the services and accommodation here, ranging from beachfront villas and cabins, to dorms, powered caravan sites and campsites. There are swimming pools, a general store, an ATM, Wi-Fi and a restaurant and bar (with happy hours daily). parksandresorts.rac.com.au/monkey-mia

01 Wild dolphins have visited these shores since a local fisherman began feeding them in the 1960s.

02 Crowds line the beach to watch the dolphins being fed.

01

Leave the crowds in your wake on Shark Bay's most remote and rugged adventure.

You know you're on a ripper of a sea kayaking trip when it tortures you with howling headwinds and low-tide portages, and yet you can't stop smiling.

Challenging conditions are de rigour for Shark Bay paddlers, but thrilling wildlife encounters quickly temper the tough times and over three to four days from Denham to Monkey Mia, you'll glide with green sea turtles, watch bottlenose dolphins hunt beneath your boat, and push off each morning through clear shallows swarming with juvenile shovel-nose rays and blacktips.

Marvel at sea snakes weaving their way through the water and watch graceful manta rays slip effortlessly past, but expect to meet Shark Bay's namesakes too. The tiger sharks that commune a day's paddle north of Monkey Mia are legendary.

02

At journey's end, Monkey Mia's popular resort village presents a savage return to civilisation, but at least you can wrap your blisters around some of the coldest beers on the coast before hitching a ride back to town.

The distance in between can be a long, hard slog, depending on the force of the predominant south-westerly winds that aid paddlers heading north then blast them when they turn south on the home run to Monkey Mia. Time your trip to make the most of winter's mild, maritime conditions (June through September) and avoid summer's strong winds and extreme (40°C+) temperatures. Plan your trip around the tides, too, or you might wake up to find your boats high and dry and the water's edge a killer, kilometre-long portage away. Ideally, you want a cycle of high morning and evening tides.

Putting a trip together is easier than you might think, especially if you bring your own expedition sea kayak, or hire one for a few weeks from Rivergods in Perth (singles and doubles from $300 per week). You might have to return your watercraft afterwards, but this trip is so good, you won't care at all. Monkey Mia's sit-on kayaks are fine for a day paddle north along the coast, but they won't accommodate all the camping gear, food and drinking water you'll have to carry with you on this adventure.

From Denham, it takes between three and four days to cover the deserted coastline that wraps around the northern tip of Peron Peninsula to Monkey Mia – all of it protected as Francois Peron National Park. If you don't want to rush, plan overnight stops at Big Lagoon, Gregories (for snorkelling) or Bottle Bay, then one last camp at Herald Bight. In between, there are pristine beaches everywhere; just be sure to leave no trace.

By world standards, Shark Bay is an incredible marine wilderness to explore, so if paddling's your thing, don't miss the grand tour. Rivergods in Perth offer a five-day tour from $1295 per person (rivergods.com.au). Alternatively, if you're wanting a short 'taster', check out local operator Wula Gura Nyinda's day tour from 8.30 am – 4.30 pm for $210 (adult) or $180 (kids 2-16) wulagura.com.au.

01 Wula Gura Nyinda offer a day tour including double kayaks and BBQ meal.

02 10 per cent of the world's remaining dugong population lives in Shark Bay.

Tackle adventures that connect you with Shark Bay's ancient past.

To travel is to learn and Wula Gura offers a swag of Indigenous-led adventures that will deeply connect you with the region, reinterpreting the local landscape and its food and fauna from an ancient, Indigenous perspective. But don't expect to just sit around the campfire (unless you've already spent the day kayaking, hiking or SUPing). Tours run by traditional owner Darren' Capes' Capewell take you to the farthest ends of Shark Bay, which in Malgana language is called Gutharraguda, meaning Two Waters.

You can paddle a kayak all day long, take a 4WD bush tucker tour or spend the night on a 'catch and cook' camping safari that will have you foraging for local food and trying your hand at the didgeridoo. 'Capes' is a bit of a legend, carrying out these tours on the same country his grandfather Murrum was born on. His knowledge about country is first-hand and real, and he's equally happy sharing it with you while you're sitting around a campfire or paddling a SUP across a lagoon at sunset.

Capes often brings along his dog Chalya, whose name in Malgana language means 'to have good energy'. Malgana language is still in the process of revival, since the last elders that spoke it passed on in the 1990s. That means on these adventures, you'll hear words and songs that might otherwise have been lost forever, and that's something you'll never forget.
wulagura.com.au

LEARN

Shark Bay is a wild, diverse and fascinating piece of Australia, and there's no shortage of things to learn.

From the captivating stories that make up Indigenous Dreaming to the distinct and unique natural wonders that confirm its place as a World Heritage-listed area, you could spend days on end just learning and listening. If that's your idea of bliss, try out these places.

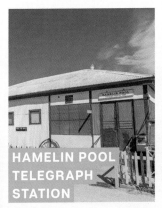

HAMELIN POOL TELEGRAPH STATION

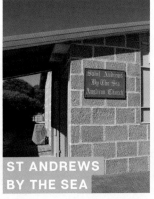

ST ANDREWS BY THE SEA

SHARK BAY DISCOVERY CENTRE

Formerly called Flint Hill, Flagpole Landing, and now Hamelin Pool, this 135-year-old telegraph station was once an essential link between Perth and Broome. Today, an intriguing little museum at Hamelin Pool Caravan Park conserves this slice of history, and you can join daily tours (from $4), devour a mean Devonshire tea, or spend the night (campsites and ensuite rooms).
hamelinpoolcaravan-park.com

Built in 1954 from coquina shell blocks quarried at Hamelin Pool, this Anglican Church is one of Denham's best heritage buildings. Locally known as the Shellblock Church, it was funded by St Andrews-By-The-Wardrobe in England and constructed of bricks hand-cut by the then rector of Carnarvon Rev. Ron Hobby and two Scottish stonemasons. Join the weekly Sunday service at 9 am to look inside, or stroll the grounds at any time.

Take a journey through exhibits showcasing Shark Bay's natural, Indigenous and pioneering history. Fill your head with intriguing facts about wildlife and conservation, and catch a screening of "Fire on the Water" – a 3D film about the 1941 battle that sunk the HMAS Sydney II. The film plays every 30 minutes and is free. Multi-day tickets to tour the centre cost $11 adults, $8 concession, $6 kids and $28 for families. Find it on Denham's foreshore.

CARNARVON AND THE KENNEDY RANGE

With a landscape so arid the rivers run underground and rocks so mammoth they dwarf the biggest in the world, this sparsely populated region offers a quintessential slice of Outback Australia. But juxtaposed against the rust-red vistas, a coastline studded with turquoise bays and pristine, white-sand beaches beckon snorkellers, surfers and sandy-footed escapees to the water's edge.

With a population of around 5500 people spread out across a region the size of some countries, travels around Carnarvon can feel a little isolated. Sandwiched between World Heritage-listed Shark Bay and Ningaloo Reef, it's all too easy for travellers to rush on in either direction, but that would be a mistake. Hidden in plain sight are some of the state's most alluring coastal camping destinations, world-famous surf breaks, conservation reserves for turtle encounters, and, did we mention the fishing?

GNARALOO
STATION

MINILYA

RED BLUFF

LAKE MACLEOD

CAPE CUVIER

BOOLOGOORO

QUOBBA BLOW
HOLES

COORALYA

BOOLATHANA

TO MOUNT AUGUSTUS
AND KENNEDY RANGE

CARNARVON

TO WOORAMEL

Carnarvon sits at the mouth of the Gascoyne River, an 865km-long enigma that rates as WA's longest, but for most of the year lies hidden, deep underground. Despite its dried-up appearance, the Gascoyne has supported Indigenous Australians for more than 30,000 years as a meeting place for five traditional language groups whose stories are stunningly told in Carnarvon's Gwoonwardu Mia Cultural Centre.

The unmistakable rock that gives Temple Gorge its name in the Kennedy Range.

Europeans arrived in the late 1800s, bringing sheep and lofty ambitions to nurture tropical fruit plantations with the Gascoyne River's mineral-rich artesian flow. A whaling station through the 1950s was later converted to process prawns, which are as abundant as the crabs, scallops and snapper hauled in today. All this food-inspired industry means that you'll dine well in Carnarvon, and the abundance of tropical produce grown on the river's fertile alluvial plains fills farm gate stalls all over town, and lures weekend crowds to Carnarvon's growers market.

Overlooking the sea, Carnarvon is a colourful hub adorned with bright murals, sculptures and fascinating art installations. It's also home to an unlikely number of museums devoted to preserving Carnarvon's recent past, from missions to the moon and maritime history to shearing, cyclones and railways too.

The wildest adventure you can tackle takes you far east to stand beneath the largest sandstone inselberg the world has ever seen world: Mount Augusta. Its smaller but equally stunning neighbour, Kennedy Range National Park, is more accessible with great bush camping and renowned for its incredible wintertime blooms of everlasting daisies.

Northwest of town, travellers pinch themselves as they gaze upon perfect Indian Ocean sunsets, staking out idyllic beachfront campsites and spending long days on the sea. Three working pastoral stations – Quobba, Gnaraloo and Warroora on the edge of Ningaloo Reef – all welcome travellers, offering rare access for surfing, diving, snorkelling and fishing, and a heavenly slice of the simple life.

STAY

Along this wild, turquoise coastline, working pastoral stations provide the best sea views, with cabins and campsites aplenty.

From secluded Quobba Station to the absolute beachfront of Warroora Station, if you can rough it just a little, you'll covet some prime real estate for pocket change. Self-sufficient waterfront campsites are everywhere, and those at New Beach and Bush Bay, 34km south of Carnarvon, cost from just $4 – $5.50 a night.

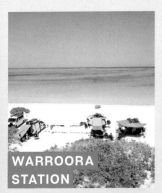

WARROORA STATION

RED BLUFF RETREATS, QUOBBA STATION

CAPRICORN HOLIDAY PARK

If you've ever seen dreamy photos of blissful campsites beside a perfect turquoise sea, it was probably here. These coveted campsites for self-contained travellers are national park-run. Our favourites are 14 Mile, The Ridge, Sandy Point and Elles Beach. Nightly fees are $8 per adult, $6 for concessions and $3 per child (book at **parks. dpaw.wa.gov.au/site/ warroora-coast**). Away from the sea, there are cottages and cabins at nearby Warroora Homestead. **warroora. com**

Quobba Station is more than just a rugged surf-camp. For a far-flung, luxury stay, Red Bluff's secluded safari tents are hard to beat. Positioned high on the cliffs, these furnished, solar-powered glamping tents cost from $250 per night, twin-share (3-night minimum) and look out over the bay. Each one has its own bathroom, kitchenette and perfect little balcony to check the surf each morning and enjoy the sunset from each evening. Book at **quobba. com.au/retreats**.

To tick off a few of the local highlights including the growers market, the Fruit Loop and the swag of interactive museums and galleries on offer in Carnarvon, you'll need at least a couple of nights close to town. Capricorn Holiday Park has a pool and offers peak-season powered sites from $46 a night or inexpensive, comfortable cabins for families and couples. Find it on the eastern side of Carnarvon, walking distance from the CBD and some great cafes. **summerstar.com.au**

Soak in natural artesian baths under a starry night sky.

Nothing soothes road-rattled bones quite like sliding into a hot tub, especially when it's full of therapeutic, mineral-rich water. Artesian pools are a surprising rarity on this coastline, but Wooramel River Retreat comes to the rescue with a quartet of small, circular pools fed by the Birdrong Aquifer. From 240 metres below ground, the water bubbles to the surface at a toasty 33 degrees – perfect for a chilly winter's night. At dawn, nothing will get you out of bed faster than the thought of having the plunge pools all to yourself.

The subterranean water is rich in magnesium, iron and salt, so while it may not wind back the clock, your skin

01

It only happens two or three times a year before sinking back far beneath the surface, but in dry times there are other things to explore. Take your 4WD on a 70km self-drive around the property, past the 100-year-old shearing shed, before returning to forage around Wooramel's most historic site – its rusting, century-old rubbish tip. Something of an open-air museum, the tip preserves pastoralist treasures like wool carts and old cars and a thousand aging, everyday items discarded since the 1800s when Wooramel Station first began.

Travellers have the Hall family to thank for drilling the artesian bores back in the 1920s, but it wasn't until the Steadman family took over in 1987 that the pools were opened to the public. Stay overnight, in the campground, in plush safari tents or self-contained unit accommodation, to enjoy the plunge pools after dark.

Unpowered sites cost $15 per person and come with hot showers and fire pits, and the station serves up a traditional Aussie camp oven dinner for $25 per head on Monday and Wednesday nights (May to mid-October, BYO drinks, cutlery and plates). To book your spot, head to **wooramel.com.au** or phone **0499 425 888**. You'll find it signposted 2km off the North West Coastal Highway, 120km south of Carnarvon.

and joints will thank you. Get your daily dose early, before the midday heat kicks in (unless you like to sweat). You can drop by Wooramel River Retreat (at Wooramel Station) just to use the pools ($5 entry) or stay overnight for the chance to see the 'upside-down' Wooramel River rise to the surface after heavy rain.

01 Relax in one of of the four artisan baths, landscaped into a small fenced in area, with water coming from 240 metres below the ground.

CARNARVON
HERITAGE PRECINCT

Four museums, 100 years of history, just one ticket.

For the backstory on Carnarvon, head to the Heritage Precinct to wander through four museums jam-packed with more than 100 years of relics that document life on land and sea.

There's a museum for every traveller, and with one ticket to cover them all, you can explore what interests you the most. Learn about Carnarvon's lighthouse keepers and shearers, meet The Kimberley – the last steam train in the northwest – and wander through One Mile Jetty Interpretive Centre.

The jetty that stretched stoically out to sea since 1899 – formerly the longest in Australia's northwest – helped turn Carnarvon into a marine transportation hub. When Cyclone Seroja blasted the WA coastline on April 11, 2021, with 170kph, category 3-force winds, One Mile Jetty didn't stand a chance. By

lunchtime on that day, the heritage-listed jetty had been washed away. But its long and significant history is on record, and the attached One Mile Jetty Café is the best place in town for coffee.

The Lighthouse Keepers Cottage Museum rekindles real and romantic tales of the mariners who safeguarded the coastline from 1900 to the 1970s. Elsewhere in the Heritage Precinct, the Shearers Halls of Fame Museum showcases the Gascoyne's 1950s shearing industry with interactive displays, old machinery.

Finally, the Railway Museum remembers Carnarvon's historical tramway, which once stretched from the centre of town to the end of One Mile Jetty. All four museums can be explored on one ticket, purchased at One Mile Jetty Café ($10 for adults, $5 for kids and $25 per family), located at Annear Place and open from Tuesday to Sunday, 10 am to 4 pm.

EAT

In a place where farming and fishing outnumber all other occupations, you can expect to eat well.

Productive fisheries haul in prawns, scallops, snapper and crabs (available fresh from the factories, May to October), and the Gascoyne River's fertile plains nurture a bounty of tropical fruits and vegetables that local chefs conjure into fantastically fresh meals.

SUNSETS CAFÉ, ONE MILE JETTY

BUMBAK'S FARM

A TASTE OF THAI

Celebrating the famous jetty swept away by Cyclone Seroja in April 2021, this café on Babbage Island teams incredible natural vistas with a fresh menu of local fare. With sea views on all sides, the vibe is relaxed and beachy, and Sunday night pizzas are served with live music amd good times. For the rest of the week, it's a top place to sip a sundowner, watching the day slip away over the Indian Ocean. For more on what's happening, find them on Facebook.

Located on North River Road along Carnarvon's scenic Fruit Loop drive, the roadside shop at Bumbak's Family Farm gets rave reviews for its tropical fruit ice-creams, choc-coated bananas and mango smoothies. There's fresh produce for sale plus a huge range of locally made jams, chutneys, dried mango and chilli sauces. Cash is the only way to pay, so bring plenty. It's open 9-4 every day or 9-3 on Sundays. **facebook.com/bumbaks**

Fon and the team cook up Thai classics with a twist, incorporating fresh Gascoyne River greens and local, wild-caught blue swimmer crabs and fish into inspired creations like Pat Pong Karee Boo (curried Carnarvon crab). All the sauces are made in-house, vegans get plenty of choice, and you can have your curry, noodles or soup as spicy as you like. Call ahead for takeaway (0409 911 198) and eat it on Carnarvon's foreshore. Located on Hubble Street. **facebook.com/atasteofthaibyfon**

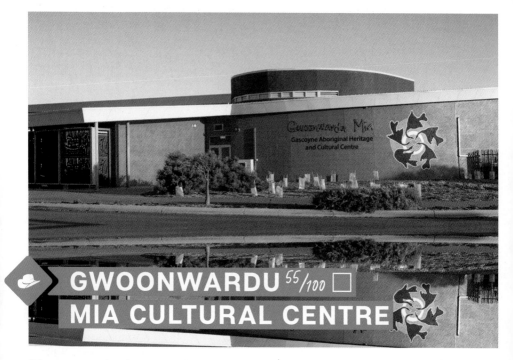

GWOONWARDU ⁵⁵/₁₀₀ ☐
MIA CULTURAL CENTRE

The stars, the bush and the Dreaming showcased in ways you'll never expect.

This interactive centre will change the way you see this part of the world, inspiring you with Dreamtime stories recorded more than 60 years ago and a time-lapsed night sky that teaches ancient Indigenous navigation by the stars. Projected onto a custom-designed domed ceiling, Gwoonwardu Mia's version of the Milky Way is a real eye-opener, and there's plenty more to explore.

Bringing together the collective wisdom of the Gascoyne's Yinggarda, Bayungu, Malgana, Thadgari and Thalanyji language groups, Gwoonwardu Mia is a welcoming place that's free to visit and fascinating. A garden of local native plants reinterprets their importance to Indigenous peoples as medicine, food and sacred ceremonial ingredients, and you can wander through the art gallery in quiet solitude or explore the centre's exhibitions and collections for $10 per adult, $8 concessions and $5 for kids.

When you go, allow time to explore the award-winning exhibition Burlganyja Wanggaya: Old People Talking – Listen, Learn and Respect, which safeguards and showcases the long-standing oral tradition of storytelling amongst the Gascoyne's Indigenous peoples. Opening times change seasonally, so head to **gahcc.com.au** before you visit.

CARNARVON SPACE 56/100 ☐ AND TECHNOLOGY MUSEUM

Play in the west's only space-age museum.

It might seem strange to find a former NASA satellite tracking here, but the coastline between Carnarvon and Perth hangs beneath a popular route for spacecraft leaving Cape Canaveral, USA. It's also the first bit of land that spacecraft see after their long passage over the Indian Ocean's deep blue.

Back in the 1960s, when the world space race was on, two tracking stations in Carnarvon helped relay Neil Armstrong's famous first moon steps to Australian and UK audiences. Ideally located, the stations played vital roles tracking and relaying communications between the Gemini, Apollo and Skylab missions, and at the height of their usefulness, employed 220 people.

Decommissioned in 1975, it gathered dust until local townspeople, fascinated by a history they'd never heard about, starting collecting relics from local sheds and backyards, including a dome that was used to construct Gwoonwardu Mia.

Housed in the OTC Satellite Earth Station, the museum contains actual equipment used at these two facilities and, best yet, lets you play with it. You can sit in a life-sized space capsule and press buttons on real-life space equipment. Kids will love it, and since they'll want to bring their parents, the $35 family passes are excellent value. Otherwise, adults pay $15, kids are $6, and concessions get in for $10. Over the peak winter months, the museum is open daily from 9-4 pm (**carnarvonmuseum.org.au**).

GASCOYNE GROWERS 57/100 ☐
MARKET AND FRUIT LOOP

Shop and eat your way along the Carnarvon Fruit Loop.

Known as the 'salad bowl of the west', Carnarvon is the place to get your hands on succulent, just-picked produce sold straight out of the fields from farm gates along the quirkily tagged 'Fruit Loop'. This scenic drive for shoppers links together roadside farm stalls and shopfronts supplying just-picked mangoes, avocados, melons and exotic fruits like black sapote and starfruit, all sold without sky-high price tags and excessive food miles.

Buzolic to thank for planting his first banana back in 1928 and kick-starting the Carnarvon food movement.

The Fruit Loop takes you out of town along North and South River Roads. Along with a dizzying abundance of organic and biodynamic veggies and fruits (especially over winter from May to mid-October), you'll find local fruits turned into more delicious versions of themselves: jams, ice creams and smoothies. Get in early to snap up the choc-coated bananas that locals rave about, found at Bumbak's on the North River Road.

Tackling the Fruit Loop is a great way to explore Carnarvon, do the shopping and fill empty bellies on board. But if you happen to be in Carnarvon on a Saturday morning between May and October, get to the Gascoyne Growers Market in Carnarvon's town centre (near the information centre). This small farmers market is all about food – fresh seasonal produce, seafood and eggs, coffee brews, baked treats, breakfast and buskers.

When you go, remember to BYO bags as the markets are earth-friendly and plastic bag-free. To find out more, visit **gascoynefood.com.au/growers-market**. From August-September, you'll catch the Gascoyne Food Festival.

The Loop is no touristy affair: Carnarvon's 1000-plus hectares of working plantations supply 70 per cent of WA's winter fruits and veggies. That includes a staggering 4000 tonnes of bananas annually and nearly 1300 tonnes of mangoes! Today's foodies and farmers have a bloke named Jack

01 Dramatic walls of colourful bougainvillea on the Fruit Loop drive.

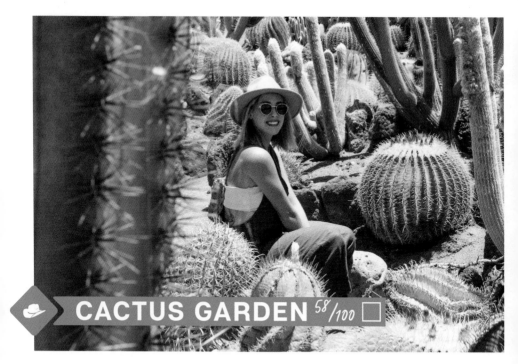

CACTUS GARDEN 58/100 ☐

The West Coast's most famous spike of prickles that bristle.

When Robert Ellis Westcott planted the first cactus in his front yard 14 years ago, he couldn't have imagined just how Insta-famous his prickly little Carnarvon garden would become. Today, the Cactus Garden is firmly on the map, luring 30-40 carloads of travellers a day to wander beneath cacti that bristle and bloom, some towering five metres high.

It might look like you're stumbling onto the set of a Wild West cowboy flick, but it's not altogether unexpected after the long, empty desert drives that are de rigueur to reach Carnarvon from any direction. Located on South River Road, it's definitely the quirkiest stop you'll make along

Carnarvon's famous Fruit Loop (page 138), and you can't miss it. The cacti have been planted right to the front verge, with a neat little pathway leading through them and, interestingly, a big whalebone behind them, leaning against a giant water tank.

Westcott is today well used to strangers wandering around his patch, and has since told the ABC that he hopes to expand his garden, no doubt to the delight of the local visitor centre who recognise this unique attraction as a tourist experience in its own right. When you go, keep in mind that this is Mister Westcott's front yard, so continuing in and onto the property without permission is trespassing. Be respectful, take nothing but pictures, and watch those darn spikes!

CHINAMAN'S POOL $^{59}/_{100}$ □ AND ROCKY POOL

Cool down, on the outskirts of town.

Flowing for 865km from the Robinson Ranges to the sea, the Gascoyne might be WA's longest river but consider yourself lucky if you see it. Its invisibility is legendary because, for two-thirds of the year, this upside-down river flows almost entirely underground. Seen or not, the mighty Gascoyne supplies enough water to irrigate Carnarvon's thirsty agricultural plots local mining operations. But, it does its best work where it flows through two waterholes; Chinaman's and Rocky Pools (pictured).

Chinaman's Pool is the easiest to reach, a 15-minute bike ride from Carnarvon's town centre. Follow any of the unnamed roads or tracks off the eastern end of Margaret Row. Fringed with old gum trees and some rope swings, this is a peaceful spot to cool off and spread out a picnic.

Further from town, travellers and wildlife commune alongside Rocky Pool, which holds water year-round. It's deep and cool, and if you search around, you might pocket river-smoothed agates or fossil washed down from the Kennedy Ranges.

If you are headed west to explore Kennedy Range National Park (page 144), Rocky Pool makes a good first stop to boil up a cuppa, get wet and watch the birds at dusk and dawn. You'll find it 55km east of Carnarvon along the Carnarvon-Mullewa Road to Gascoyne Junction Road.

KINGSFORD $^{60}/_{100}$ □
SMITH'S MAIL RUN

01

Follow the world-famous aviator's outback postie run.

In 1924, the world was changing, and even remote West Australian outback towns along the Gascoyne River weren't immune. WWI had finished, bringing with it industrialisation, motor vehicles and bounding opportunity, if you could recognise it. Little-known commercial pilot Charles Kingsford Smith certainly could. Long before he was knighted for his world-famous aviation feats, he and mate Keith Anderson started the Gascoyne Transport Company,

introducing trucks on a route previously dominated by camels and drays.

Carting mail, sheep drovers and station cooks along a rugged track west of Carnarvon to the Bangemall Goldfields near Mt Augustus and all the way to Meekathara, Smithy's Run was a constant, slow struggle along barely-there paths. The round trip took the pair two weeks. Thankfully today, the most scenic stretch of the 800km-long Kingsford Smith Mail Run is sealed, although diversions en route create adventures for 4WD travellers.

The first 240km from Carnarvon to the Kennedy Range follows the mighty Gascoyne's 865km-long underground river. Along the way, 19 interpretive sites share anecdotes from Kingsford Smith's time on the mail run, Dreamtime stories and the region's colonial history. You can stop for a swim at Rocky Pool (page 141), spot rare, timid wildlife on the Doorawarrah claypans, and if engineering feats get you excited, marvel at the spot where the Dampier-to-Bunbury gas pipeline crosses the road, linking 127,000 sections of pipe.

Outside of Gascoyne Junction, jettison any old shoes you have on board at the famous roadside "Boot Camp", best done by standing well back and flinging your boots by their laces onto the tree branches. Beyond the Boot Camp,

the track turns north past historical remnants of hand-paved roads and across the Gascoyne River to some shaded riverside picnic spots.

Although unsealed, a well-graded track detours into Kennedy Range National Park that bristles with wildflowers over the late winter months (August and September). Back on track, the mail run continues to the Old Bangemall Inn at Cobra Station, where you can fuel up and spend the night, visits Mount Augustus National Park and winds up in Meekathara, where Smithy's job was finally done.

01 Crossing over the Gascoyne River.
02 The famous roadside 'Boot Camp', outside of Gascoyne Junction.

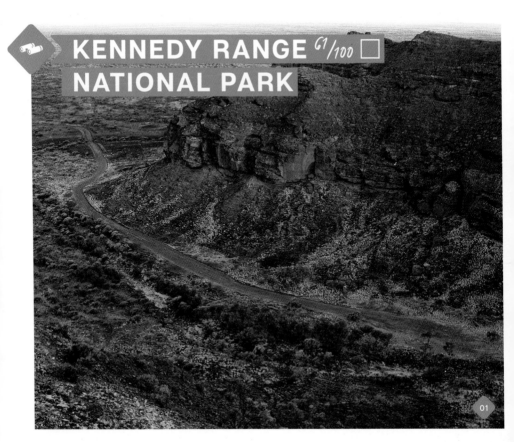

KENNEDY RANGE
NATIONAL PARK

01

Discover hidden petroglyphs, sacred pools and a towering mesa girthed by wildflowers.

Far from the sea, in a red-sand desert that bristles with wintertime wildflowers, this stunning red rock mesa beckons you inland to hike its crumbling canyons and discover hidden rock pools and ancient petroglyphs. Fringed with precipitous cliffs and rising 100m above the Lyons River valley plains, Kennedy Range is a massive, flat-topped plateau, 75km long and up to 25km wide.

Known as Mundatharrda to traditional Inggarda guardians, this entire range was once buried beneath an ancient sea, forged from iron-rich sand and shale that, thanks to some pretty spectacular uplifting, elevated this mammoth plateau to tower above the plains. Deeply eroded and sculpted by strong winds and wild summer rains in the millions of years since, this island of rock is a fascinating canvas, scored with narrow chasms that run with waterfalls and cradle rock pools long into the dry season.

What you'll love about this big red rock is what's hidden from sight, and all the short walking trails and rock-hopping adventures that tempt you deep into its rugged folds. Throw in some starry night camping with nothing but the after-dark howl of dingoes to soothe you to sleep, incredible wildflowers to photograph, and unlikely animal encounters at shady waterholes, and you'll quickly realise that this vast, empty landscape has some pretty significant pulling power.

Located 240km from Carnarvon along sealed, then graded gravel roads, Kennedy Range is accessible to 2WD travellers. And because it's situated about halfway to Mount Augustus National Park (page 148), you can plan one big inland adventure and tick off adventures to WA's best and biggest rocks!

Winter is the ideal time to visit, when cool, comfortable temperatures favour hiking, and wild creatures are drawn to drink at the last waterholes lingering on the plains.

Steep cliffs dwarf Kennedy's Temple Gorge Campground at the base of the plateau, and although there's nothing but toilets and plenty of flat ground, the views are as incredible as the stargazing.

A camp host is usually in place from May to September, but campsites must be booked online at **parks. dpaw.wa.gov.au** ($11 per adult, $7 for concessions, and $3 per child). Gather firewood on your approach to the national park and strike it aglow at the communal firepit in the centre of camp.

From Temple Gorge Campground, you can walk or drive to trailheads at three incredible gorges, and tackle the Escarpment Trail to the top of Kennedy Range for endless, lofty views (class 4, 3.4km, 1.5-3hrs return). Look closely as you explore Drapers Gorge to discover its amazing rock petroglyphs and sit beneath timeless fig trees shading small rock pools. The trail pushes up and around a seasonal waterfall for impressive views over the plain before reaching a large rock pool and ledges where we discovered the skeletons of euros (kangaroos) and feral goats (class 4, 2km, 1.5 hours return).

A shorter adventure takes you into Temple Gorge. Follow the rock cairns from the campground along the creekbed to a fork in the gorge presided over by The Temple – a prominent rock feature that looks like nothing else. From here, head left for 100m to the waterfall that flows in the wet, retrace your steps and explore the other boulder-strewn canyon to reach the rock pool at the head of the gorge (class 3-4, 2km, 1-2hrs return).

On the western side of the range, high clearance 4WD vehicles can explore further along the Gascoyne River and discover ancient springs flowing from the rock that have long nurtured wildlife, Indigenous peoples and pioneer-era pastoralists.

01 Giant cliffs of iron-rich sand and shale create an awe-inspiring vista, especially at sunset.

HONEYCOMB GORGE, 62/100 ☐
KENNEDY RANGE

Hike the chasm with the most dazzling rock canvas on the coast.

Of all of the discoveries you'll make at Kennedy Range, Honeycomb Gorge is the most intriguing. Follow the short rocky trail from the carpark to the spectacular amphitheatre of mesmerising, pitted rock formations eroded into the cliff face. You'll know, instantly, why it's got its name.

Coastal winds and seasonal waterfalls soaking salt into the rock have sculpted the bizarre patterns of cavities in the cliff face. Over time, the salt crystallises in the rock's pores, loosening it enough to be carved into intricate patterns by the wind. The setting sun ignites this rust-red mosaic with dazzling light, and the small, shady pool at the head of the gorge is a lovely place to be at day's end.

From the Honeycomb Gorge carpark, the walk to the pool takes just 10 minutes each way (class 3, 600m return). Alternatively, you can reach the gorge on foot from Temple Gorge Campground. Skirt along the base

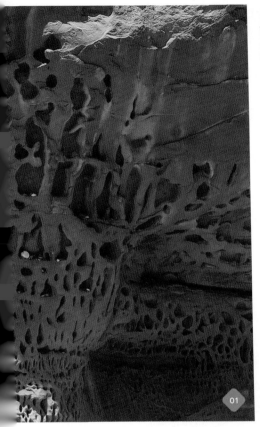

cornflowers underfoot. The wildflowers alone – especially the great blazes of fuzzy purple mulla mullas – make the months of August to September the ideal time to discover Kennedy Range, but you'll appreciate the cooler temperatures at that time too.

of the escarpment's brilliant cliffs through acacia scrubland of wattles, grevilleas and spinifex grasses, and a boulder-field of fallen rock, much of which contains ancient marine fossils. Walking as the day cools down, you're likely to see euros, splendid fairy-wrens and perhaps a dingo too (class 3, 5.8km, 3-4.5hrs return).

To Indigenous Inggarda guardians, Mundatharrda (Kennedy Range) remains an intensely spiritual place. The mythical water snake kajurra inhabits many of the park's waterholes, so treat all pools with respect, and steer clear of restricted Indigenous heritage sites.

After heavy winter rains, around 80 species of annual wildflowers burst into colourful bloom and in many places, you can't walk without crushing papery everlasting daisies and bright blue

01 This unique rock face has been sculpted by winds and seasonal waterfalls.

02 Fuzzy purple mulla mulla flowers bring colour to the red dirt during wildflower season.

Move over Uluru, meet this Big Rock rival.

If you thought Uluru was the biggest rock in the world, climb its WA rival to stand atop a giant sandstone inselberg that's two-and-a-half times bigger than the Red Centre's pride and joy. The Wajarri people call it Burringurrah, and it's enormous in every way: 1106 metres tall and covering a whopping 4795 hectares of red desert. You'll find it 465km east of Carnarvon, which is a pretty long way to travel to see a big rock, but this one won't keep you grounded.

Unlike Uluru, you can climb Mount Augustus all the way to the summit. It's not easy, but that's exactly why you'll want to tackle the challenge: five to eight hours of rough, steep, hard yakka (class 4, 12km return). If you're keen, set out on the trail at first light so that you can be on your way back before the sun gets hot and high. Temperatures on this trail get sky-high over the blistering summer months (September to March), so save this adventure for winter, carry plenty of drinking water and wear sun-smart clothing, including a hat.

Of the many characteristics that separate Uluru and Augustus, this perhaps is what sets them apart: Uluru is a monolith and the world's largest at that, a single formed rock, sitting on the plains. Mount Augustus is a many-layered sandstone beast that protrudes from the earth's crust in one fantastic fold, rising as an island mountain or what's more accurately known as an asymmetrical (lopsided) anticline. Its sandstone is older than Uluru too, but like Uluru, Augustus (or Burringurrah) is the subject of incredible Dreamtime storytelling.

The Wajarri tell of a boy who, after fleeing his initiation ceremony in the desert, arrived at this spot. He was speared in the leg and hit over the head, and when he fell and died, his tall shape transformed into Burringurrah. The name 'Mount Augustus' came in 1858 when explorer Francis Thomas Gregory climbed the rock during his 107-day Gascoyne region expedition. He is credited with being the first European to have done so, and named the rock after his brother, Augustus Charles Gregory.

This sacred rock is etched with many ancient petroglyphs, and you can access them via short trails at Mundee, Ooramboo and Beedoboondu along the 49km scenic loop drive around Mount Augustus. It's 2WD friendly and leads to lookouts, swimming holes and rock caves too. From Carnarvon, Mount Augustus is a 465km drive, suitable for 2WDs despite the gravel road after

Gascoyne Junction. Remember to slow down and carry a spare tyre in case yours fall prey to sharp, jagged rocks.

If you like to hike, you'll find plenty of well-marked trails accessed off the 49km drive circuit, including the Flintstone – Beedoboondu Rock Trail with its age-old Indigenous rock engravings (class 3, 500m, 30 mins return), and the Saddle Trail at the Pound where stockmen once held cattle on their walk to Meekatharra (class 3, 1km, 20-60 mins return). To cool off, head to Goolinee (Cattle Pool), a permanent waterhole on the Lyons River.

To take in a stellar sunset, Emu Hill showcases the ultimate vista over Mount Augustus, and early the next morning, Yalaweerie lookout is the place to be at sunrise. To plan your trip and download a park guide with hiking information, head to **parks.dpaw. wa.gov.au**. No camping is permitted in the national park, but close by, pet-friendly Mount Augustus Tourist Park provides twin rooms from $88 per night, powered campsites from $40/couple/night, and unpowered sites just $15 per person (kids under 11 years stay for free, (**mtaugustustouristpark.com**).

The prime time to visit is between June and September when temperatures are coolest, but remember that outback nights can drop to near-freezing, so pack your fleece trackies, thick socks and plenty of warm bedding.

QUOBBA BLOWHOLES 64/100 □
AND CAMPING RESERVE

Sky-high blowholes, secluded snorkelling and sandy, coastal camps.

The Indian Ocean swell that relentlessly pummels Quobba's rust-red cliffs stops travellers in their tracks, blasting through blowholes that shoot 20 metres high. This startling scene thrills onlookers, drenching too-close daredevils with its spray, and when the tide's coming in, it's immediately evident that the King Waves Kill sign should not be ignored. There are about 20 to 30 blowholes around Point Quobba, all equally perilous, and the best time to ogle them is just before high tide.

Incongruously, just a kilometre away, these same steep sea cliffs crumble onto a pretty, white-sand beach that arcs around a cerulean lagoon. The locals call it 'The Aquarium' because just offshore, a submerged wall of reef and rock holds back the swell, calming the lagoon for snorkellers who float over colourful coral bombies and eyeball luminous fish.

Beyond this scene, beachfront campsites are carved into the sand dunes, tucked amongst a rambling sprawl of old beach shacks with incredible access to the sea. In good weather and calm seas, locals fish and

dive south of the beach boat ramp, off the reef near Black Point. Down on the sand, rough-hewn shade shelters protect kids building sandcastles and parents letting the real world slip out of mind.

This idyllic, bare-basics camp has a long history of facilitating great sandy escapes and prices here some of the most affordable on the coast: $11 for adults, $8 for seniors and pensioners, and nothing for kids under 16 years. Campers need to carry a chemical toilet on board and BYO water, but there are dump points and bins, and generators and dogs on leads are permitted.

Bring snorkelling gear and fishing rods, and SUPs and surfboards if you can squeeze them in, and enough food to settle in for at least a few nights.

Pay your fees with cash to the on-site camp host or by credit card at Carnarvon's information centre. You'll find the camp located 75km northwest of town, 1km south of the Blowholes, where the bitumen empties you onto a long stretch of isolated beaches and reef-fringed shores. From Quobba, a graded road pushes north to Quobba Homestead (2WD accessible) before rattling on to Red Bluff and Gnaraloo Station.

Witness the world-famous Bluff Barrel in action.

Some surfers spend their whole lives chasing a wave as good as Red Bluff's world-famous Bluff Barrel. Others camp out on this remote West Australian sheep station, bewitched by the sea and waiting for the swell to find them. But while Red Bluff's solid left-hand point break is what clearly put this rustic surf Mecca on the map, it's not only surfers who flock to its sandy camps and safari tents.

Located on Quobba Station at the end of a seriously bumpy access road, Red Bluff's endless white sand beach is breathtaking and pristine. Although

facilities are scarce, the beachfront Red Bluff Store serves up lattes, mango milkshakes and gourmet pizzas, and the lofty, luxurious safari tents betray this camp's off-the-grid status.

Here you'll meet Monique Durant, who arrived at Red Bluff back in 1995 and, together with husband Reid, transformed the tiny, timber Red Bluff Store into the kind of laidback seaside hangout where you can sip a brew with sandy feet and watch the sun set over the surf. They built a completely self-sufficient home up on cliffs and, in the process, raised and home-schooled eight Red Bluff grommets. With a four-hour return trip to the nearest supermarket, Monique is a master of

and rolling over a reef break to form the legendary Bluff Barrel. Ride this epic lefthander that flings you triumphantly out across the bay, if you dare, or have fun on the gentler swell that crosses the bay. Even if you don't brave the waves, watching from the shade of a sea cave is better than anything streaming back in the big smoke.

Accessible by 4WD, you'll find it 138km northwest of Carnarvon via Quobba Blowholes (allow 2hrs). Arrive with your own beds on board, or treat yourself to a safari tent stay from $250/night (3-night minimum). The camp is pet-friendly, and the spacious, unpowered campsites come with fireplaces and pit toilets ($20 per adult, $8 per child, free for under 4s). Centrally located, the store serves good coffee, basic supplies, simple meals and plenty of ice creams and snacks to fuel energetic surfers. Plan your stay from June to August, and bring drinking water and wood.

simplicity, and her unclouded love for the Bluff's invigorating seascape is intoxicating.

Red Bluff's campground is remote and entirely off the grid – no power, showers or flushing toilets – but it's the fact that nothing much (except the espresso machine) has changed in two decades that makes it so appealing. There is excellent fishing, a fine arc of sand to beachcomb and, further afield, boaties can access fringing coral reefs and historical wreck dive sites.

Red Bluff's flattop finger of rock stretches seaward at the southern end of the bay, interrupting the swell that peels off its point and sending it curling

If off-road travel is not an option, nearby Quobba Homestead provides 2WD-accessible shacks (from $90/night) and campsites with power, showers and drinking water from $22/person. It's the headquarters of a century-old sheep property with 80km of spectacular shoreline and fine catches of dart, tailor, trevally, snapper and mulloway up for grabs. While it lacks the appeal of far-flung Red Bluff, it makes a sensible base camp if you don't think your rig will survive the hour-long rattle north (**quobba.com.au**).

GNARALOO STATION 66/100 ☐

Come for the camping, stay for the turtles, ride the swell.

At the very southern tip of Ningaloo Marine Park, Gnaraloo epitomises the beachside, pastoral station camping experience that Western Australia does so well. For 65km along the coast, turquoise waters wash onto secluded sandy shores backed by vibrant, red desert cliffs. But while the vistas are stunning, it's what you can do here that pulls travellers far off the bitumen.

Vibrant coral reefs enthral snorkellers, anglers and surfers equally, with calm, sheltered snorkelling sites, offshore fishing holes and plenty of surf breaks too. At spots like the famed Tombstones, long-period Indian Ocean swells roll perfectly over reefs, creating waves that surfers travel from all over the world to experience, and non-surfers line up on the shore to watch in awe.

You can set up camp at Three Mile or the Homestead, checking into beachfront campsites and earthy stone cabins set along the cliffs (from $20/ adult, kids half price). There are hot showers, toilets and a shop, and it's not

turtle watching sessions, observing the turtles as they stoically lumber ashore to dig their nests and lay their eggs. You'll help to collect vital data (egg temperatures, turtle measurements and tag numbers) and help build a better picture of the turtles' movements and nesting rates. At Gnaraloo, strict turtle encounter guidelines are in place to ensure that turtles are not disturbed by light and noise and spooked back into the sea before egg laying is completed.

only intrepid travellers who are drawn to this stretch of coast.

Each year between October and March, thousands of loggerhead and green sea turtles come ashore to nest. Turtles are encountered just about every night, and so significant are these nesting sites that Gnaraloo Station devotes a portion of all accommodation fees to turtle preservation.

If you visit over summer, between October and February, you can join national park rangers on all-night

There are lots of reasons to get to Gnaraloo, located 150km north of Carnarvon, so book your stay well in advance at **gnaraloostation.com**, or contact the station on **(08) 9942 5927**.

01 65 clifftop, unpowered campsites run parallel to the sea at Three Mile Camp.
02 Between October and March, thousands of loggerhead and green sea turtles visit Gnaraloo to nest.

CAPE RANGE AND NORTHERN NINGALOO

It's difficult to fathom the astounding diversity and abundance of life that flourishes along Australia's largest, fringing coral reef. Stretching for 260km, remarkably close to the coast, Ningaloo is revered amongst sea lovers for harbouring the best shore-based diving, snorkelling and marine wildlife encounters in the entire country.

The largest aggregation of whale sharks ever documented in the world takes place annually on Ningaloo Reef: 300 to 500 bus-sized beauties whose grace and patience bewitches swimmers every winter. Only on Ningaloo can you keep pace with humpback whales and manta rays, spot dugongs and sharks, and witness the lifecycle of four sea turtle species as they hatch, nest and mate along the clearest of turquoise bays.

The food chain that feeds it all is equally spectacular: 700 species of vibrant reef fish, 600 crustacean species and 300 corals whose annual full moon spawning brings the reef to life. All this magnificence might be enough to lure travellers to Cape Range's rustic, seaside camps, but out of the water where Cape Range rises across stark, waterless plains, extensive karst systems harbour an underground wonderland of rare, significant cave fauna and deeply flowing watercourses.

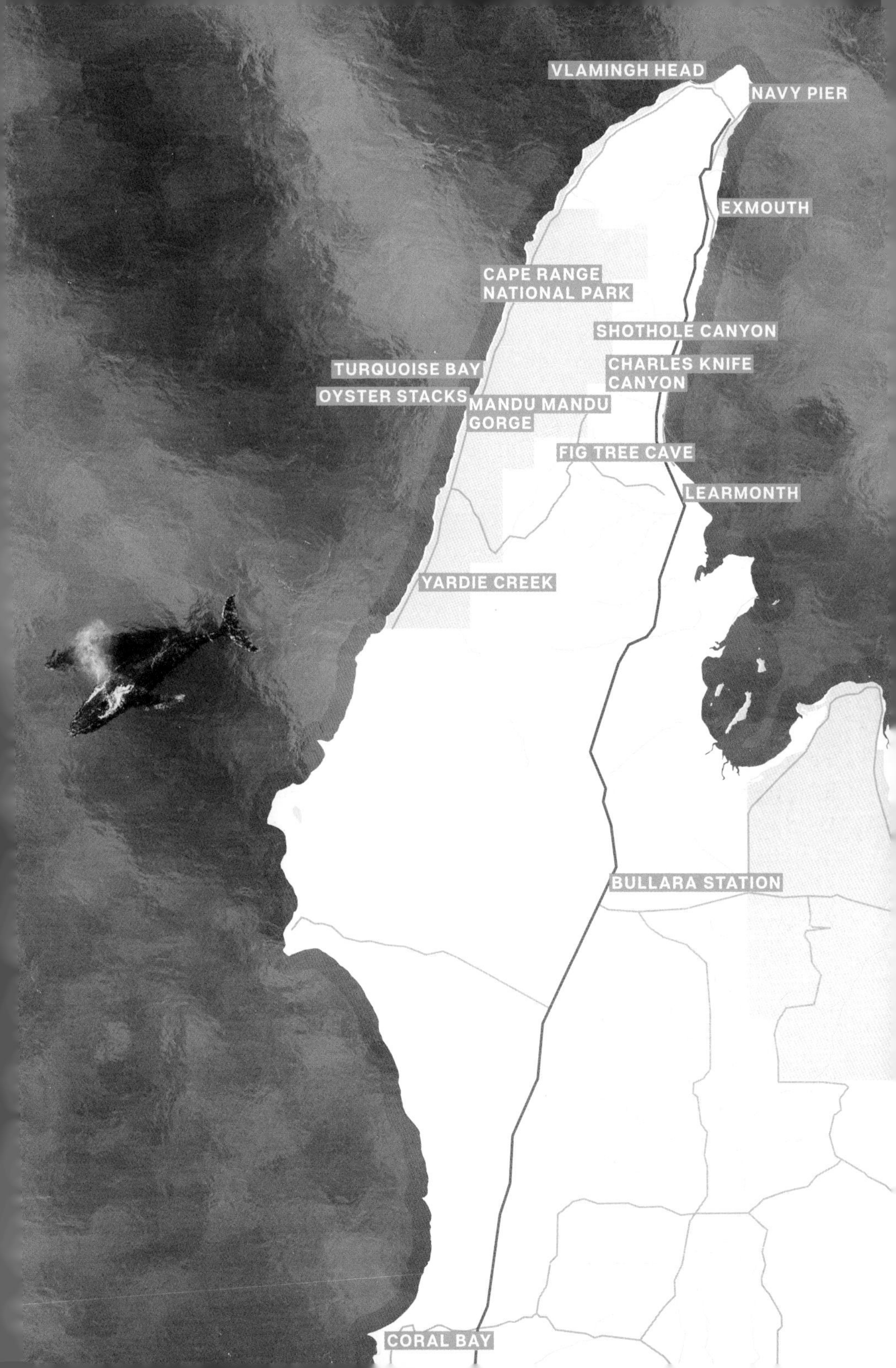

VLAMINGH HEAD

NAVY PIER

EXMOUTH

CAPE RANGE
NATIONAL PARK

SHOTHOLE CANYON

TURQUOISE BAY

CHARLES KNIFE
CANYON

OYSTER STACKS

MANDU MANDU
GORGE

FIG TREE CAVE

LEARMONTH

YARDIE CREEK

BULLARA STATION

CORAL BAY

The Baiyungu people call this place Nyinggulu, meaning 'nose', for the cape's protruding shape. Their 35,000-year-old occupation of Cape Range lingers in caves where stone artefacts, shell beads, marine mollusc shells and bone fragments have been unearthed.

But perhaps what's most outstanding about this arid, remote and isolated region is the dazzling to-do list of outdoor adventures you get to indulge in. Long-time locals know that you could never squeeze it all into a single visit, which is why they park a boat in their driveway and use it to sneak off to secret spots every chance they get to surf, dive, fish and explore their way through Ningaloo's endless bucket list.

But living in Exmouth is not for the faint-hearted. Rain falls less than 20 times a year, the sun shines 320 days out of 365, and over summer, temperatures blaze at a white-hot 45°C. Almost nothing grows in Exmouth, and supplies of everything except fresh seafood has to be transported huge distances. Yet this tight-knit community thrives on their simple, salty lifestyle, acutely aware of how special Ningaloo is and highly engaged in safeguarding it from ever-growing tourism, overfishing, and oil and gas interests.

Incongruously, Exmouth is home to the Harold E. Holt Naval Communications Station (a joint US-Australian centre) and the RAAF's Learmonth Air Weapons Range, which, although maintained as a bare-base with no units in residence, has the potential to run military exercises and bombing practice.

But in a town where people adapt their lifestyles just to live somewhere awesome, you can expect to be surprised. No one does it tough here (there are two fantastic breweries, for starters), but you won't find shopping malls and fast food outlets. Instead, you'll spend your cash at laidback wholefood outlets and chef-owned eateries, you'll shop with bare feet and salty hair and you'll take your tours with locals who are deeply passionate about Ningaloo.

And there's a lot to get excited about. Ningaloo's incredible marine diversity made it a shoo-in for world heritage listing, and a dizzying range of tours can help you encounter it all. But it doesn't cost a fortune to get a dive mask on your face, step off the beach and see it for yourself. Cape Range National Park specialises in primitive, beachfront camping with easy access to snorkelling sites and walking trails, surf breaks, boat ramps, offshore kayaking moorings, and turtle watching tours.

You don't have to rough it to enjoy it all, either. There are plenty of places to stay that keep your sheets sand-free, and enough rental options to put together your own independent adventures to the offshore Muiron Islands, 4WD-only campsites south of Yardie Creek, and fishing trips in a surprising number of locations off the Ningaloo coast.

STAY

From bare-basic campsites to remote five-star glamping, stays on the Ningaloo coast please all kinds of travellers.

Exmouth and Coral Bay's laidback resorts and holiday parks keep things civilised. Over the popular wintertime travel season, Exmouth locals listing spare rooms on Airbnb provide comfy beds and some great travel tips, too.

CAPE RANGE NATIONAL PARK CAMPING

STATION STAYS

SAL SALIS

Occupying prime real estate where Ningaloo Reef sweeps close to the shore, these national park campsites suit self-sufficient travellers keen on daily swims and seaside happy hours as the sun goes down. Facilities are basic – just toilets and picnic shelters – so BYO everything, including some shade, and cling to the fact that from your rustic, beachfront nook, the water's edge is just a quick skip over the sand. Sites cost $11 for adults, $8 for concessions, and $3 for kids, but book well in advance. parks. dpaw.wa.gov.au

For a taste of station life, head to Bullara Station (above), famous for its 'coffee and scones' and the happy hour campfires that gather travellers together (and fill them with free damper). Book a room in the Shearers Lodge, the Hale Hut or a campsite. bullarastation.com.au. Giralia Homestead, south of town on the edge of the Exmouth Gulf is a favourite with fishos. Choose homestead or budget rooms or riverside or 4WD-accessible beachfront campsite from $15 per night. giraliahomestead.com.au

Go off-grid at Sal Salis Eco Safari Camp, located in the dunes along Ningaloo Reef. With zero phone reception or internet access, you'll have no choice but to slow down and soak up your surroundings: snorkelling the reef, gazing up at the night sky and reading good books. Nestled in the dunes, 15 solar-powered safari tents all come with ensuites, gourmet meals, sunset wine and canapés and as much kayaking, reef time, and guided gorge walks as you can handle (from $849 per person, per night). salsalis.com.au

01

For close-to-the-reef stays and wild underwater adventures.

Boasting straight-off-the-sand snorkelling, resort accommodation and lots of reef adventures, Coral Bay is a lively holiday hub with a rare proximity to the southern end of Ningaloo Reef. Its ever-expanding cluster of cafes, shops and holiday rentals appeals to everyone's indulgent streak. Although it lacks lonely beachfront campsites and lofty gorge walks (you'll find them 200km north in Cape Range National

Park or just south in Warroora Station), almost all that you can do on Ningaloo Reef, you can do in Coral Bay.

Start with a snorkelling or dive adventure to tick off swims with Ningaloo's Big 3 – manta rays, whale sharks and humpback whales. There are fishing charters and sunset sailboat cruises, and you'll need at least a few underwater sessions to fully explore snorkelling sites at Bill's Bay (find Ayre's Rock 300m out from the northern end of Town Beach), the staghorn coral gardens 500 metres south at Purdy Point, and to swim with turtles at Five Fingers Reef, 4.5km south and accessible by 4WD or your tinny. Five Fingers Reef is shallow and perfect for beginners and kids, and it's the best place close to Coral Bay to snorkel with turtles.

A short walk north of Bill's Bay, the sanctuary at Skeleton Bay nurtures up to 200 juvenile blacktip reef sharks from October to March. At its southern end, a shallow pool known as The Aquarium teems with life, safeguarding a colourful 'fish soup'. If you have a 4WD and seek seclusion, follow the Coastal Access Track 15km north to the Bateman Sanctuary Zone to snorkel at Oyster Bridge, the shimmering Lagoon and Five Mile, a reliable spot to eyeball enormous coastal manta rays with a wingspan of up to 4.5m.

Drifting and diving and dazzling you with their curls and turns, manta rays are harmless filter feeders that will dwarf you with their size and leave you awestruck as you glide together, finning against the undertow. On a lucky day, you might chance an encounter with the elusive, 7m-long oceanic manta ray, but your best bet for such a thrill is aboard a tour boat that takes you further offshore (priced from $185 to $250 per person).

Out of the sea, the Coral Bay Walk Way leads to coastal lookouts above the playgrounds of dolphins and mantas, and from Yalobia Lookout, you'll spot mobs of emus and kangaroos roaming the scrubby plains south of town.

There is no shortage of places to rest your head in Coral Bay on any budget. Ningaloo Reef Resort, Ningaloo Coral Bay and Peoples Park offer everything from beach chalets and resort rooms to backpacker dorms and caravan sites. The 4WD Coastal Access Track leads to primitive camping areas in Nyinggulu (Ningaloo) Coastal Reserves and takes well-prepared off-roaders on a wild ride all the way north across tidal Yardie Creek to Cape Range National Park.

01 Follow the Coastal Access Track to Oyster Bridge for fantastic snorkelling and swimming.

02 Swim with these graceful angels of the sea in Coral Bay.

WHALE SHARKS 68/100 ☐
ON NINGALOO REEF

Swim with the biggest fish in the sea.

Is it a whale, or is it a shark? The world's biggest fish is a baffling enigma, but despite filter feeding like a whale, the whale shark's bone-free skeleton classifies this gentle giant as the largest shark on the planet. Whale sharks are synonymous with Ningaloo Reef, and their wintertime aggregation off Exmouth has been documented as the largest in the world.

Their length may be daunting – anywhere from 3 to 18 metres – but whale sharks are perfectly safe to swim alongside as they suck krill, plankton and small fish into their enormous, five-foot-wide mouths stacked with 300 to 350 rows of tiny teeth. What lures them close to the coast is Ningaloo Reef's mass coral spawning in March and April every year. It begins five to 10 days after the full moon, and this fleeting, three-day buffet that feeds the marine food chain is a dazzling time to be underwater.

Sizing yourself up against a whale shark is a euphoric experience and a big deal on Ningaloo Reef. First, a spotter plane takes to the skies, alerting boat crews down below who make a beeline for the whale sharks and drop snorkellers into the path of the oncoming creature,

ten at a time. The process is highly regulated to protect both sharks and swimmers and allows you plenty of precious minutes with the whale shark in between much-needed breaks to catch your breath and smile.

While whale sharks are well protected in Australian waters, these world travellers are afforded no such guarantees elsewhere on their journeys where they are routinely caught in fishing nets, dying onboard as by-catch, and as a result of boat strikes and starvation caused by ingesting floating plastic rubbish as they feed close to the surface.

The IUCN Red List classifies them as endangered, but it's not too late to rally in support of whale sharks. Choose to encounter whale sharks with a tour operator that strictly adheres to the rules, allowing them to swim freely, and better yet, directly donates to their conservation.

Day-long whale shark tours run from Exmouth and Coral Bay on both ends of Ningaloo Reef, and cost from $295 (kids) to $445 per person. There are too many good tour companies to mention, but Trip Advisor recommendations can guide you to the best fit in making a choice.

01 Each whale shark has its own unique pattern, much like a human fingerprint, which makes it individually identifiable.

02 Whale sharks are protected in Australian waters and the tourism industry is strictly regulated.

SWIM WITH ⁶⁹/100 ☐ HUMPBACKS

Whale-watch underwater with these majestic songsters.

WA's annual humpback migration is the world's largest: 30,000 whales all cruising to the warm breeding grounds in Australia's northwest. And Ningaloo Reef is one of the few places in the world where you can swim with them.

While whale sharks swim slowly, humpbacks move at a hastier pace, often outpacing the swimmers hoping for close encounters. Only about 70 per cent of the time will your humpback swim work out (it's 100 per cent for whale sharks), but when it does, you'll bag an experience that's unforgettable.

Humpback whales are spotted along Ningaloo Reef from June to November, but swimming tours from Exmouth and Coral Bay (where the outer reef is closer and quicker to reach) operate throughout August, September and October. Expect to pay around $430 for a day tour, or $150 to join the trip as a non-swimming observer.

The process for spotting humpbacks is pretty much the same as for whale sharks. A spotter plane radios the location of slow-moving or resting pods of whales to the tour boats, and when they intercept them, swimmers are dropped in the water around 30 metres from the whales. Given that humpbacks grow to 17-metres long, it's like swimming with a block of apartments!

One of their fiercest natural predators is the orca, which often hunts newborn calves. Spotting the occasional orca is an unexpected bonus to a day underwater on Ningaloo Reef, and you might chance an encounter with a whale shark or one of the reef's year-round residents, the enormous manta ray.

SURF

It's unlikely to get a mention as a surf travel destination, but Exmouth pulls in some decent swell. Mid-winter (July) is the prime time for surf, when the easterlies are blowing, however the influx of tourists and the limited number of beach breaks means things can get crowded. Local surfers will drop whatever they're doing when the swell's on. Have a chat, keep the vibes high and enjoy the wildlife encounters surfing the world's largest fringing reef.

Beware of urchins when you're paddling out: watch where the locals are paddling out and stay on your board for as long as possible on the paddle back in. Help protect Ningaloo by wearing plenty of reef-safe sunscreen and keeping the beach plastic-free.

DUNES

Also known as 'Surfers Beach', Dunes is an exposed reef break with left- and right-handers, about 20km north of Exmouth via Mildura Wreck Road. Dunes is best suited to competent surfers rather than beginners and fires up on a mid-tide between July and October. Arrive early in the day to snag a spot under one of the wooden shelters, which provide the only shade on the beach, otherwise BYO umbrella.

HUNTERS

Driving west, just past the turn-off to Vlamingh Head Lighthouse, Hunters access road leads to this good fun right-hander that's suitable for beginners and advanced surfers too, depending on the size. Wind is off-shore with some south or south-east in it. It's also a turtle rookery, a nice bonus on clear days when turtle heads pop up around you. Like Dunes, Hunters is best between July and October.

WOBIRI

About 20 minutes' drive out of Exmouth and 500m south of Jansz Beach, Wobiri is a fantastic beginners' beach break with a sandy bottom, gentle waves and shallow water where the wave breaks. Plenty of the local surf schools run lessons here, or you can rent a soft board from Exmouth Surf Centre ($25/half-day) if you want to learn on your own. exmouthsurfcentre.com.au

FIG TREE CAVE 70/100 ☐

Drop down the ladder into Exmouth's secret cave.

Hidden on the edge of Cape Range National Park, about 45km from Exmouth, this daring little caving adventure is one of Exmouth's best-kept secrets. It's a top spot to discover in between hikes and scenic drives on the eastern side of Cape Range, and descending Fig Tree Cave's seven metre-long, loose-hanging steel chain ladder will send a shiver up your spine.

To get there, drive 30 minutes south of Exmouth on Minilya-Exmouth Road and, using Google Maps to guide you, turn off near the airport onto a bumpy, unnamed 4WD track. Drive about 30 minutes more until you spot the low-lying fig tree that obscures a well-hidden hole in the ground. Here, a wobbly ladder leads you straight down into the cave through a narrow entrance, following the fig tree's roots all the way to the cave floor.

Inside the cave's cool, dark interior, you'll discover impressive stalactites, stalagmites and columns, but it's for the thrill of the descent that you'll want to unearth this adventure. Arrive at midday when the sun is overhead to dramatically illuminate your photos, and wear sturdy boots and a head torch. Keep a watch for snakes, too and tread carefully because your phone won't get reception here if this adventure goes pear-shaped.

If you're up for more fun, there's another cave further up the track plus another 700 caves and dolines throughout Cape Range National Park. Almost all these caves have a vertical drop to gain entry, so come prepared. With no signage guiding you to the cave, your best bet is to search 'Fig Tree Cave, Learmonth' on Google Maps and make your way there from the airport.

LEARN

Learning's a bit more hands-on around Cape Range, so step outside and have a go at scuba or free diving, kiteboarding or even surfing.

Discovering a new water-based skill on the world's longest fringing reef just makes sense, and there's no shortage of ways to explore.

FREEDIVING LESSONS

How long can you hold your breath underwater? The clear waters of Ningaloo are perfect for freediving, and you can learn to breathhold for longer with ocean advocate Liv Rose. Start from scratch on a three-day PADI Freediver Course, grow your skills on a four-day advanced course, or join a multi-day expedition. The courses combine theory with water time in the pool and out on the reef and are a must-do for anyone who wants to take their snorkelling skills to greater depths (from $599). Learn more at livforthesea.com

NINGALOO AQUARIUM AND DISCOVERY CENTRE

It's an interpretive centre, and aquarium rolled into one, with heaps of history to unearth and even a cyclone room! The aquarium tanks display an astounding number of fish, coral and other marine species you'll spot while snorkelling the reef, and you'll learn plenty about Cape Range's hardy echidnas, emus and euros. Here's where to come if you want to learn everything you need to know about Ningloo's World Heritage status. It's open seven days, tickets cost $19 adults and $14 kids or concessions. ningaloocentre.com.au

LEARN TO FLY A MICROLIGHT

Spot for sharks, whales and manta rays as you glide over Ningaloo Reef, turning inland to swoop and soar over the crumbling canyons of Cape Range National Park. With your hands on the controls and the wind in your hair, you'll feel as free as a bird, and at all times, safe, accompanied by your trusty instructor. A microlight is basically a three-wheeled hang glider with a giant propeller. An introductory flight with Exmouth company Birds Eye View gets you airborne with no experience necessary (from $229). birdseyeview.net.au

BADJIRRAJIRRA ⁷¹/₁₀₀ ☐ TRAIL

Peer from knife-edge lookouts into WA's own Grand Canyon.

High above the ocean, scored deep into the eastern flank of Cape Range National Park, Charles Knife Canyon lures walkers with rugged scenes of crumbling limestone walls and yawning valleys, caves and sheer cliffs – all of it rosy at sunset and resplendent when wildflowers bloom.

Named after Charles Knife, a 1950s oil prospector, this canyon is wider and wilder than you could possibly imagine, but with Ningaloo tugging for everyone's attention, few people dedicate a morning to put themselves

in the midst of this incredible landscape. You don't have to walk it – there are drive-to lookouts, or you could see it from the air on a microlight flight – but if you do, you'll find yourself on one of the Coral Coast's best and most surprising wanders.

Winding along the edge of steep, crumbling canyons, across vast spinifex-covered ridges and down through gullies and small gorges, the Badjirrajirra Trail leads to staggering viewpoints of Shothole Canyon, enormous and alluring across the plateau (6.8km, 3hrs return). The loop trail is rocky and rugged, and utterly wild, which is exactly why you'll want

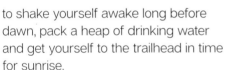

to shake yourself awake long before dawn, pack a heap of drinking water and get yourself to the trailhead in time for sunrise.

What makes this Class 4 adventure a challenge is the heat. In December 2012, a 14-year-old Scottish boy died on the trail during extreme 48°C summertime temperatures. The lesson here is to tackle this walk only during the cool winter months, and set out as early as possible to avoid the midday heat.

To get there, follow the Exmouth-Minilya Road 22km (20 mins) south of town, turn onto Charles Knife Road and drive about 11km to the top of the range to reach Thomas Carter

Lookout. The access road is a mix of bitumen and graded gravel that's fine for conventional vehicles, and the walk trailhead is located at the car park. At 311m, Thomas Carter Lookout showcases grand vistas that are more than worthy of the long, scenic drive, especially in the early morning when sunrise over the Exmouth Gulf sets the canyon walls aglow in rosy, golden hues.

01 Begin your walk at the Thomas Carter Lookout at sunrise, to beat the heat.

02 Not up for the walk? Pack a picnic and set-up at the lookout to enjoy breathtaking views down into the gorge.

SHOTHOLE CANYON

4WD into the wild, wild west.

The name alone screams 'Wild West', and bumping along the pothole-ridden road into Shothole Canyon, you'll feel like you've entered the set of an American western. Sunk into the friable limestone of Cape Range, Shothole Canyon is a cavernous sight: vast and wide and bounded by gently sloping ridges that flare skywards, capped by towering, mesas with sheer, ruby-coloured cliffs.

The scene becomes even more imposing during wildflower season when the best of 600 species bloom across the range (August to October). The canyon is named for the shot hole scars it bears; the remnants of explosive charges set off in the early 1950s by oil explorers in Cape Range.

In the cool hours of day, emus emerge, and echidnas hunt for food, and the howls of dingoes echo through the valleys in the lonely hours after dark.

With no long walking trails to tackle, Shothole Canyon is a mediative place to visit in the early hours or upon dark, to watch the sun cast its colours in wild spectacles and then steal them back as it disappears over the range.

A 4WD vehicle is recommended to tackle the long, corrugated access road. To find it, head 17km south of Exmouth on the Exmouth-Minilya Road, take the Shothole Canyon turn-off and continue on the gravel for a bumpy 12km.

At the end of the road, there are picnic tables, a toilet and a steep, 100 metre-long staircase that elevates you to a lookout over the canyon with just a few minutes of sweaty walking (Class 4, allow 15 minutes). Sunrise views over the Exmouth Gulf are best, and if you arrive at dawn, carry a thermos of coffee and a jacket to ward off the early morning chill, and don't forget your camera. It's impossible to take a bad photo here.

EAT

Despite its remote location in a region far too arid for anything useful to grow, Exmouth has a surprisingly fresh food scene with excellent restaurants and creative menus.

Cafes, such as the Beach Shack at Bundegi Beach, epitomise what eating out in Exmouth is all about: fresh ingredients, original dishes, rustic vibes and views that capture fantastic scenes of the North West Cape. As good as camp-cooked meals can be, budget a few nights out in Exmouth, and you won't be disappointed.

ADRIFT CAFE

THE SOCIAL SOCIETY

WHALEBONE AND FROTH BREWERIES

Tucked away in Houston Street, Exmouth, Adrift specialises in 'simple, rustic, fresh food made with love'. It practically never closes, so head here from 8.30 am to fuel up on eggs and rostis or to lunch on burgers, wraps and vego salads. It's fully licensed (and stocked with local Exmouth brews), and the dinner menu is deliciously heavy on seafood (don't miss chef Matt's seafood linguine or the coconut and Szechuan pepper calamari). adriftcafe. com.au

Known by locals as 'SoSo', this wholefoods cafe in the centre of town serves good coffee, fresh-pressed juices and the kind of food that gets vegans and vegetarians very excited. This solar-powered café practices what it preaches, and if you bring your own cup and containers, you'll get a discount on takeaways. There's free Wi-Fi and a bustling crowd, so get in early. SoSo is open 6.30 am to 2 pm weekdays, and closes 1 pm on the weekends. Thew Street. facebook.com/ thesocialsocietyexmouth

Exmouth has two working breweries. First up, Froth's beach-styled beer oasis teams craft brews with beer-of-the-day battered seafood, gumbo and some creatively fresh vego options. It's open daily, from 11 am until late (frothcraft.com). Whalebone is all about unwinding: eating good, woodfired pizza, working your way through craft beers and kicking back to live tunes. It's open 4 pm daily. whalebonebrewing. com.au

NINGALOO'S LAGOON

Freedive, float and boat across this giant, natural aquarium.

What sets Ningaloo apart from other reefs is that it's a fringing reef. This means that the reef is close to the coastline, which creates a long, shallow lagoon on the beach side of the reef.

Beyond the white sand shorelines, Ningaloo's lagoon is crammed with coral bombies and marine life. The two to four metre depth provides a calm sanctuary to explore the sea without venturing out far. The lagoon's shallow depth means that you're never too far from the surface to snatch a breath.

Exmouth has a large community of freedivers, and it's a skill you can hone with freediving instructor Liv Rose, who offers three-day beginner courses from $599 (livforthesea.com).

There are plenty of places to snorkel straight off the beach, such as Oyster Stacks (page 177), but for intrepid freedivers and snorkellers, venturing further out into the Lagoon via kayak, SUP or tinny will allow an escape from the beach crowds.

Pack your kayak with snorkelling gear or rent one from Exmouth Adventure Co from $30 per half-day (exmouthadventureco.com.au). There are kayak-only white moorings positioned above deeper snorkelling sites at Bundegi, Tantabiddi and Osprey Sanctuary zones, all about 400m offshore.

You can launch a boat from Tantabiddi Boat Ramp, just north of the national park entry station, or hire one from Exmouth Boat Hire exmouthboathire. com.

DIVE THE ⁷⁴/₁₀₀ ☐ NAVY PIER

Flash your ID to access this highly restricted dive site.

It's one of Australia's best shore dives, and the only one under a US-Australian naval base. Located within Exmouth's Naval Communications Station Harold E. Holt, the 300 metre-long Navy Pier is hallowed ground for divers, and access is only permitted when you book with Dive Ningaloo, and verify your identity with Australian Federal Police on arrival.

If it seems like a lot of trouble to go to for a jetty dive, consider just what's growing down there: kaleidoscopic soft corals and sponges that attract immense schools of reef fish – butterfly, angel and parrotfish – all buzzing about a backdrop crowded with garish nudibranchs and pocketed with secretive moray eels and octopuses.

Sea snakes and sharks dart about too, wobbegongs and placid grey nurses. There are big schools of snapper and trevally, and a giant Queensland grouper called BFG in just 15 metres of water. Photographers and macro divers will love this spot, even if the visibility is restricted to between three and ten metres, thanks to the strong, nutrient-rich currents that feed the marine life.

Dive times are entirely dependant on the tide. To verify your identity, you'll need to present Australian Federal Police with a valid passport or driver's licence, and if you forget it, you won't be let in. Divers under 18 years need to supply a copy of their ID to Dive Ningaloo at least two days prior. Exmouth Navy Pier is located at Point Murat (follow Murat Road north of town). Contact diveningaloo.com.au.

Whale watch where eagles soar from this historical sunset spot.

When humpback whales move into Ningaloo, Vlamingh Head Lighthouse provides ideal high ground to watch their offshore antics. Wedge-tailed eagles soar over the landscape that's so vast and flat, you can watch both sunrise and sunset from the same historical spot.

After the tragic shipwreck of the cattle steamer SS Mildura in 1907, the call went out for Exmouth's first lighthouse to be built. Work began in 1909, but it took three years to complete.

Visible up to 22 nautical miles (41km) offshore, the lighthouse's kerosene lamp kept two lighthouse keepers busy, while living in isolation at their lofty, lonely spot. Provisions of food and fresh water were infrequent, delivered by steamer from Fremantle to Exmouth then horse-drawn carriage, or carried overland from Onslow by camel.

The lighthouse keepers' cottage remains today, maintained by the nearby Lighthouse Caravan Park, but the light was replaced in 1969 by a brighter beam from the US Naval Base in Exmouth. Today, it's the luminous sunrises and sunsets that gather locals and travellers to Vlamingh Head. Don't forget your binoculars during the whale season (June to November).

Beneath the lighthouse, the long sandy beach at Lighthouse Bay is a popular spot for a swim, and if you've got a longboard, you'll get a thrill riding the small wave that often wraps around the headland. Over the summer months, look for turtles nesting or hatching here.

CAPE 76/100 ☐
RANGE TURTLES

Encounter turtles up close, on land or at sea.

Sea turtles steal the spotlight over summer when they return to their birthplaces at Cape Range. Thousands of green, loggerhead and hawksbill turtles – known by their Baiyungu name as Majun – gather from September.

They come to mate, tumbling in the breakers and taking time out to rest on the shoreline in clear view of awestruck onlookers. It's a revealing spectacle rivalled only by the night-time, nesting marches that follow, Females come ashore to dig up to 10,000 nests and lay their eggs from November to February.

All summer long, tiny hatchlings emerge to scurry to the sea, and you can watch them hatch on Turtle Eco-Education Tours, held February to March. Book in advance at the Milyering Visitor Centre or the Ningaloo Visitor Centre ($25 adults, $10 kids, $60 families), and meet your guides at the Jurabi Turtle Centre. Turtle nesting tours also run from December to February (6.30-9 pm).

You might be lucky enough to spot nesting turtles on your own, but be sure to give turtles plenty of space, remain silent and keep torches switched off. To find out more, visit Jurabi Turtle Centre, an interpretive shelter signposted between Hunters and Mauritius Beaches at the tip of North West Cape.

Australia is home to six of the seven turtle species – all classified as endangered or vulnerable. Summer is the best time to swim with them, especially around the beaches south of Vlamingh Head Lighthouse and also at the Muiron Islands (page 182).

TURQUOISE BAY 77/100 ☐

Snorkel Ningaloo's famous Drift Dive

The north-flowing current that sweeps snorkellers effortlessly across Turquoise Bay's famously blue lagoon reveals stunning underwater scenes. Spot timid reef sharks sheltering under rock ledges alive with nudibranchs and bright Christmas tree worms, blue-spotted lagoon rays nestled on the seabed, and much-admired anemone fish darting in and out of their soft, sticky homes.

The reef here flourishes exceptionally close to the shore. From the Turquoise Bay car park, all you have to do is skip across the sand, walk 100 metres south, dive in and lift your fins. Kick out over giant coral bombies to join the mesmerising, swirling procession of marine life colouring Ningaloo's

underwater canvas, scattering iridescent parrotfish in your bubble streams.

The reef's roll call of inhabitants is impressive at Ningaloo: 300 coral species and more than 700 species of reef fish, and it's here that you'll likely swim alongside the solitary green sea turtles that rise slowly from their resting places down on the sand.

A drift across Turquoise Bay only takes around 30 minutes, floating in the current that pushes you steadily north to a sandbar where you'll need to fin swiftly back to shore or risk being sucked out to sea. If the current appears or feels too strong, stick to the southern end of the beach, where there are dozens of big coral bombies to explore or head for the calm lagoon to the north. Time your drift dive for when the tide is high.

THE OYSTER $^{18}/_{100}$ ☐
STACKS AND LAKESIDE

Snorkel two of the best sites on the reef.

Ningaloo's undersea wilderness allows the easiest of access for snorkellers, and the colourful aquarium beneath the Oyster Stacks is one of the best sites on the reef. It's located just south of Turquoise Bay, where massive schools of fish shelter beneath oyster-clad sea stacks at high tide. Corals and clams are abundant, and because it's shallow, the visibility is fantastic.

The Oyster Stacks is signposted off Yardie Creek Road. Enter the water at the end of the access track and swim south to explore the oyster stacks or fin north across a stretch of reef that's popular with green sea turtles. Visit when the wind is light, an hour either side of a high tide of at least 1.2 metres.

When you go, reef shoes are handy to help you navigate the oyster-clad rocks to access the water.

Another favourite snorkelling site is the sanctuary at Lakeside, located just south of the Milyering Visitors Centre and marked by buoys close to shore. From the car park, walk to the water's edge and head south along the beach for 500m before entering the water.

Convenient for snorkellers staying on the reef, the campsites closest to Lakeside (Tulki Beach) and the Oyster Stacks (shady North Mandu) are some of the quietest in Cape Range National Park. Small and perfect for peace-loving snorkellers, they provide nothing but toilets and breezy sea views, but camping here puts you right in the action and costs $11 a night, $7 for concessions and just $3 for kids.

Spot emus and euros from this crumbling red rock canyon.

Away from the sea, across the arid spinifex plains, bright orange Sturt's desert peas bloom each winter, luring early-morning walkers high onto Cape Range. Past spindly bloodwood trees, this excellent, short hiking adventure follows a rocky, ancient riverbed deep into Mandu Mandu Gorge before scaling its rugged northern ridge and returning along the canyon's crumbling rim.

It's named for the prominent white layer of limestone that colours its cliffs, which the Baiyungu people call mandu, and renowned for grand viewpoints that, with a swift, stiff climb, elevate walkers high above the Indian Ocean. In the cool hours of day when wild things roam the endless plains at your feet, you'll likely spot euros and flocks of emus emerging from their shady resting places in search of food.

Rated Class 4, this top little leg-stretcher is best tackled at either dawn or dusk, but you can't beat the stellar sunsets from the top of the gorge, watching the sun ramp up its light show over the

Indian Ocean. If you linger for sunset, remember to pack a torch for the return trip to the car park (1.5hrs/3km).

Archeologically famous, a rock shelter discovered along Mandu Mandu Creek in the 1980s was found to harbour more than 500 stone artefact, shell beads, marine mollusc shells and bone fragments that point to the 35,000-year-old Indigenous occupation of the area stretching back to the Pleistocene era.

Mandu Mandu Gorge is signposted 15km past the national park's Milyering Visitor Centre along Yardie Creek Road.

Slow down and take great care while driving through the national park at dusk or dawn when euros appear suddenly and cross your path without warning. Wear suitable footwear and prepare for some rock scrambling, and if you need to cool down after your rocky adventure, head to the nearby Oyster Stacks or take the plunge at Turquoise Bay.

01 Follow the rocky riverbed deep into the gorge before ascending up to its northern ridge for grand viewpoints.

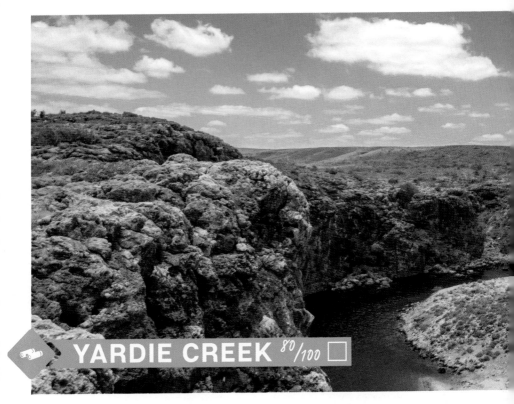

YARDIE CREEK *80/100* ☐

Paddle in search of elusive black-footed rock wallabies.

Holding the only permanent water in Cape Range National Park, Yardie Creek is a peaceful place to dip a paddle, forging upstream in search of the black-footed rock wallabies that stake out rocky ledges on the canyon's sheer walls. These well-camouflaged beauties grow to just half a metre high and only reveal themselves in the cool hours of day.

Launch your kayak or SUP at day's end when the sun setting west throws gloriously golden light across Yardie's sheer red rock walls, revealing the wallabies as they emerge to feed. Yardie Creek is also home to sea eagles whose vast stick nests stud towering cliffs, and great flocks of corellas that heckle paddlers as they approach.

If you don't bring a boat to Exmouth, you can rent one in town or join Yardie Creek Boat Tours on an hour-long interpretive cruise up the creek's tidal reaches. The tours feed you with all kinds of intriguing flora and fauna facts, and depart from Yardie Creek's jetty at 11:00 am and 12:30 pm during the peak winter months (adults $40, concessions $35, kids $20). From Exmouth, it's a 90-minute drive via sealed roads to the

jetty, or you can grab a ride with Yardie Creek Boat Tours ($40 return).

You can also hike the high trail above Yardie Creek, treading along the northern edge of the gorge to a spot where rock wallabies rest (2km return). A shorter wander, the easy Yardie Nature Walk reaches a fantastic lookout showcasing exceptional sea views (1.2km, 40mins return).

Right by the creek and just 80m from the beach, the national park-run Yardie Creek Camp provides ten sites, a toilet and a boat ramp for the bargain price of $11 per person ($3 kids). When the

swell's up from July to October, there's a nice left-hander reef break here, accessible via a short boat ride.

While Yardie Creek marks the end of the road for those without a 4WD, serious off-roaders can brave a treacherous low-tide crossing to tackle remote, sandy tracks all the way south to Coral Bay. The mouth of Yardie Creek is notorious for swallowing 4WDs, so get the tide right, pick a shallow path and have your recovery gear ready for your buddies to roll out. Just across Yardie Creek, national park campgrounds at One K Camp and Boat Harbour promise a slice of blissful seclusion.

MUIRON ISLANDS 81/100 ☐

Dive, snorkel and surf off Exmouth's own island sanctuary.

Girthed by an extraordinary, coral-fringed marine reserve, 15km off the very tip of Ningaloo Reef, the Muiron Islands (pronounced Myoo-ron) are the stuff of dreams for adventurous divers and snorkellers. Famous for their brilliantly coloured soft corals (and the turtles that feed on them), these protected waters harbour huge gorgonians and plate corals, and the thrill for divers and freedivers are all the swim-throughs, overhangs and windows in the reef wall.

In all, there are 26,000 hectares of watery paradise to explore, and divers rave about the Cod Hole off South Muiron, a deep reef cleaning station crowded with golden cardinalfish, giant potato and coral cods, and at year's end, gliding manta rays. The macro diving is fantastic, and depending on weather conditions and the amount of plankton (aka whale shark food) in the water, visibility ranges between five and 20 metres.

Top dive sites include The Spit (up to 18m depth), Whalebone and Keyhole (both on the western side of South Muiron), the drift dive between the islands at

The Gap, and the shallow coral gardens at Dinner Plates on the eastern side of South Muiron which is suitable for snorkellers too. Currents are strong off the islands so if you don't feel confident, book a day trip with one of Exmouth's dive companies (priced from $250 for two dives or $180-195 for snorkellers).

Protected as one of 20 Pilbara inshore island nature reserves, the Muiron Islands act as important nesting rookeries for flatback, green, hawksbill and loggerhead turtles, and for up to a million migratory wedge-tailed shearwaters, so the wildlife watching out of the sea is equally insane.

Camping is allowed on the north-eastern section of South Muiron Island, so if you are feeling adventurous, grab a national parks' camping permit, snorkelling gear and surfboards, and load up your boat in Exmouth and escape. There are no facilities on the island, so BYO everything, including a fuel stove for cooking (no campfires).

A rental boat capable of reaching the islands costs around $300 a day, and you can book a camping permit by phoning the parks and wildlife service in Exmouth on (08) 9947 8000.

KARIJINI NATIONAL PARK

It's not easy to turn your back on Ningaloo's tricoloured shoreline, but when you do, the Pilbara's vast spinifex plains lure you inland to the very edge of the Hamersley High Plateau. Here, far from the ocean across a sea of red dirt, twisting waterways plunge dramatically over sheer cliffs and walkers shed their shoes to explore a rosy labyrinth of slender chasms and follow watery trails to hidden, fern-fringed pools.

In this sculpted red rock playground, seven rugged gorges await discovery, and leisurely paths lead to vertigo-inducing lookouts where you can watch the sun begin and end its passage across the Hamersley Range. Traditional custodians – the Banjima, Yinhawangka and Kurrama people – call these rugged ironstone hills Karijini, and the winter thunderstorms that break over the range trigger great spears of purple mulla mulla to flower at its feet, colouring the Hamersley's foothills with a sea of bright purple blooms.

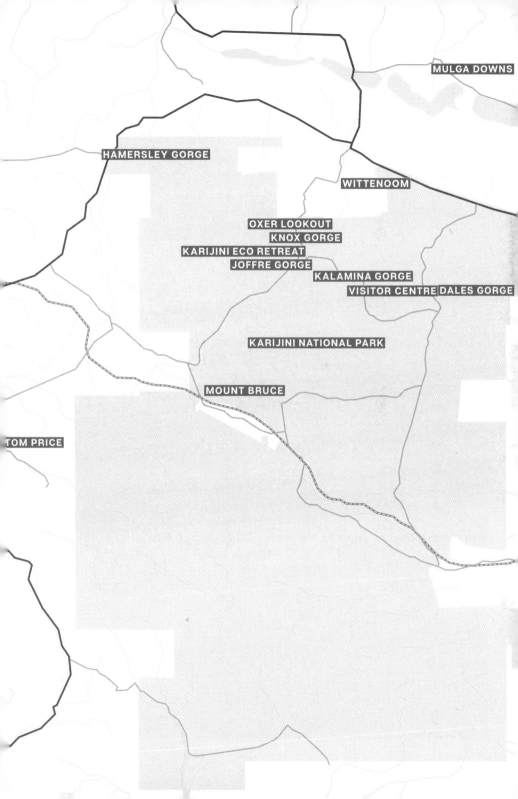

Towering high, Mount Bruce's magnificent summit elevates hikers to WA's second-highest viewpoint, and Karijini's reputation as a rock-hopping haven lures thrill-seekers in droves. Heart-pumping wet-walks through Weano and Hancock Gorges turn hiking on its head, enticing adventurers to shimmy along rock ledges, 'spider-walking' their way to leap into tantalising, 'dare-you' plunge pools.

The park's unconventional, rock hopping trails might have you thinking that Karijini is a destination for dare-devils, but there are all kinds of ways to enjoy it, and some of the best vistas are within easy reach. A sealed pathway to Junction Pool Lookout lets you peer deep into the airy abyss below, and the water's edge at Fortescue Falls is just a 400 metre-long walk away.

Easy to reach, enigmatic Hamersley Gorge is resplendent at sunset when its buckled, banded walls glow golden, and you can take it all in from a car park lookout, or scramble into the gorge to discover the Grotto and Spa Pool hidden far upstream.

However you explore, this sacred rock sanctuary is the best the Pilbara has to offer and detouring from Exmouth to Karijini and onto Millstream Chichester National Park, is an excellent way to loop back to the coast at Karratha. As WA's second-largest national park, Karijini packs a whole lot of adventure into its park boundaries, so allow at least 3-5 nights to get gorged out and soak in as many waterholes as you can.

STAY

Most travellers who stay in Karijini bring their own beds.

Bush campsites at Dales Campground are cheap and basic, but if that's not you, rest easy! Karijini Eco Retreat soothes non-campers with luxurious safari tents (with ensuites), restaurant meals and a breezy sunset bar.

DALES CAMPGROUND

SAVANNAH CAMPGROUND

KALGAN POOL

Here you're just a quick walk to the edge of Dales Gorge and the three main attractions in eastern Karijini – Fortescue Falls, Circular Pool and Fern Pool. The spacious, unpowered bush campsites suit all sizes of caravans and camping setups, and come with access to pit toilets and picnic tables. Generators are permitted at some sites, but there's no running water or showers, so bring enough to last your stay. For peak season (wintertime), book well in advance ($11 adult/night, $7 concession/night, $3 child/night, 5-16 years, **parks.dpaw.wa.gov.au**

In Karijini's west, this campground run by Karijini Eco Retreat offers unpowered sites with facilities that are a cut above those at Dales. There's drinking water and solar-powered hot showers. For bush-style luxury far off the grid, upgrade to one of the Eco Tents, which come with real beds, attached ensuites and decks where you can sit and watch the set over the endless, Pilbara plains. Another perk is that you can eat and drink in style at the Eco Retreat, and kids up to 12 years old stay for free. For details, visit **karijiniecoretreat.com.au**

If you're continuing your inland adventure after Karijini, the mining town of Newman is home to one of the Pilbara's best campsites; Kalgan Pool. Nestled within the Ophthalmia Range, this campsite has a deep pool for swimming in and a stunning banded-iron gorge backdrop. Access is strictly 4WD along a corrugated road, with some deep water crossings and plenty of potholes. Drop into Newman Visitor Centre to obtain a permit, pay via gold coin donation, to get directions and to check current road conditions. Pets allowed.

DALES GORGE 82/100 ☐
AND CIRCULAR POOL

01

Dip your toes into Dales' most perfect pool.

Teetering above the abyss at Dales Gorge, watching the plunging waterfall fill fern-fringed Circular Pool far below, hikers ponder all the ways they can reach the trio of tranquil pools at their feet. A full lap through spectacular Dales Gorge is a stellar choice for energetic explorers, setting out from Three Ways Lookout and dropping down the steep, rocky staircase to Circular Pool.

At this popular, picturesque spot, maidenhair ferns feed on the waterfall's mist and fig trees plant their roots amongst iron boulders. Springwater seeps from horizontal rock layers, and in the early hours, when Circular Pool can be all yours, you can slip quietly into its jade-coloured oasis and picnic beneath the paperbarks, dangling your feet and watching the sun ignite the rock walls all around.

Afterwards, retrace your steps and tackle the stiff climb back out of the gorge, or

02

go with the flow, rock-hopping creekside beneath fractured red cliffs to reach Fortescue Falls and Fern Pool, an hour's walk away at the other end of Dales Gorge. A full loop reveals the best that the gorge has to offer, so allow three hours or more to enjoy the icy swims, warm rock slabs and wild things at play (3km, class 4).

Less ambitious and easier to tackle, a sunrise swim at Circular Pool is a great way to kick-start your day (800m, 2hrs, class 4), but there are more options still!

From Three Ways Lookout, the gentler Gorge Rim trail takes the high road, winding beneath the shady snappy gums, desert bloodwood and cork trees that stud the edge of Dales Gorge. The kilometre-long trail ends at Fortescue Lookout where you can drop back down to shed your shoes and cool off beneath Fortescue's gentle cascades.

01 Visit Circular Pool in the early hours of the day to have it all to yourself.

02 Enjoy a dip in the impossibly-blue Dales Creek on the walk from Circular Pool to Fortescue Falls.

FORTESCUE FALLS *83*/100 ☐

01

Swim beneath Karijini's only permanent waterfall.

A flurry of whitewater fills Karijini's most popular swimming hole, spilling over two tiers of weathered rock terraces and cascading into a tranquil, emerald pool. It's sunny, spring-fed and flows all year 'round, and because it's also the easiest pool in the park to reach, Fortescue Falls is reliably flanked by plenty of swimmers, stretched out on sunny rock slabs, warming themselves in between chilly dips.

Don't let the idea of crowds put you off though. Arrive early, and you'll most likely have this icy pool all to yourself, for crowd-free bliss and first-light photos. By the time the sun appears overhead, walkers arrive too, taking in lofty views from a lookout high on the gorge rim. It takes less than 30 minutes to drop down to the water's edge, but leaving Fortescue Falls is a lot harder to do. Pack drinks and snacks, and allow plenty of time to swim and warm up again on the short walk beyond to Fern Pool.

01 Take in the view from the top lookout or walk another 30 minutes down into the gorge.

FERN POOL 84/100 ☐

01

Peer through the curtain waterfall that fills this sacred women's place.

Luring explorers 10 minutes beyond Fortescue Falls, this idyllic, turquoise pool known as Jubara is a sacred place for local Indigenous women. As significant to them as Mount Bruce is to their men, it's revered as the dwelling place of the Dreamtime Creation Serpent, who rested in Jubara after carving out waterways between the Pilbara and the sea.

Rockhop into the cool cavern behind the falls to peer out through the watery veil then, following the traditional custom,

enter the pool quietly by gently sliding in, sucking some water into your mouth and spitting it back into the pool as a sign of reverence.

Fringed by paperbarks that support a colony of flying foxes, Fern Pool is deep and clear and an inspiring place to swim, but out of respect to Indigenous customs, any ledge-jumping antics are frowned upon. To reach Fern Pool, follow the short trail that leads on from Fortescue Falls (10-15 minutes each way).

01 Slip quietly into the pool from the timber platform and enjoy some time in the peaceful cavern behind the waterfall.

KALAMINA GORGE *85/100* ☐

02

Bathe beneath Karijini's own 'Window in the Rock'.

A short scramble over Kalamina Gorge's rocky, spinifex-covered edge lands you in Karijini's most easily accessed swimming spot. Head upstream to dangle your feet beneath the falls, bathing in shallow rock pools and watching noisy reed warblers feeding on insects at the water's edge.

At dusk and dawn, insects flitting through the mist beckon birds whose hum and chatter reverberates off the steep rock walls, fractured into towering stacks of weathered red tiles. But as lovely as the pools are, there's another

side to Kalamina that will lure you far downstream. When you can bear to pull yourself out of the pools, a trail of sorts leads you on, crisscrossing the gorge around shallow pools and fallen boulders to reach Rock Arch pool and a remarkable window in the rock that few travellers see.

Rock Arch Pool marks the turn-around point, but the peacefulness of this secluded place will have you dragging your heels. For reasons unknown, Kalamina Gorge seems to attract far fewer walkers than elsewhere in the park, making it an ideal destination for solitude seekers (3km, 3hrs return, class 3).

01 Kalamina is one of Karijini's least visited gorges, so you'll likely have it to yourself.

02 Bathe in shallow pools beneath towering cliffs.

03 Kalamina is Karijini's most easily accessible swimming spot.

KNOX GORGE 86/100 ☐

Forge your own path on this wet and wild adventure.

Scramble down the rugged talus slope to the bottom of Knox Gorge and follow the watery trail that ebbs swiftly away, sandwiched between soaring, sheer walls. Paperbark trees bent horizontal by the water's turbulent wet season flow dip their feet into clear tempting pools, which will happily stall your progress through the gorge.

Waterfalls here dry up when the wet season ends, but there's plenty of water underfoot to navigate over the cool winter months, and the lack of a true trail leaves you free to make your own way downstream. Shuffle over smooth river slabs, shimmy along ledges and wade through shallow pools, switching from one bank to the other to reach a breathtakingly steep canyoning drop-off that marks the end of your walking adventure.

Allow about 30 minutes to reach this spot where the gorge walls close in to just a few feet, but much more time to float in the tranquil pools on the return journey and absorb the energy that resonates off the rock (2km, 3 hrs, class 5). Knox Gorge is a top choice for trekkers looking for wild, exhilarating wet walks, and sunsets witnessed from its lofty lookout colour a remarkable vista of the junction where Knox and Wittenoom Gorges meet.

01 Enjoy sunset from the lofty lookout.

JOFFRE GORGE 87/100 ☐

01

Stand inside Karijini's grand amphitheatre.

Carved by a thundering, 50 metre-high waterfall that all-but disappears with the last of the wet season's rains, the grand amphitheatre at Joffre Gorge offers surprising scenes not found elsewhere in the park. Take in big picture vistas from the lookout that overhangs the gorge, or scramble down its rocky ledges to reach the amphitheatre's sandy riverbed far below.

The plunge pool beneath the falls is predictably cool, deep and clear, and a soak here helps steel yourself for the short, steep hike back up to the top. A myriad of birds and the sunlight shifting overhead both create colourful scenes at the amphitheatre and, although you can't explore too far downstream, an hour or two devoted to this walking adventure is well worth it.

Drive directly to the Joffre Gorge car park to tackle the 3km return hike (allow two hours), or set out from Karijini Eco Retreat, another kilometre away. Arrive at sunrise or sunset for stunning lookout vistas (100m, 10mins return, class 2).

01 Come straight after the rain if you'd prefer to see the waterfall in full flow.

KERMITS POOL 88/100 ☐
IN HANCOCK GORGE

Straddle gorge walls on Karijini's thrilling Spider Walk.

Karijini's most thrilling wet-walk will have you splashing and climbing along a rocky obstacle course, delving deep into the centre of the earth. At class 5, it's no walk in the park, but don't be put off tackling this slippery jaunt if you are fit, agile and prepared to get wet.

The fun begins at Weano Recreation Area in the park's west where long steel ladders drop you into the gorge and onto a swiftly flowing 'trail' to the Amphitheatre. Take in the pretty waterfall

as you remove your shoes and prepare to tackle the Spider Walk, bracing your bare feet against the highly polished rock in a crazy scary stance. Shimmying along above the stream is not as difficult as it appears, and it's guaranteed to get your heart pumping!

A deep, water-filled chasm swallows the path ahead, so splash on through it to reach the lurid green Kermits Pool. Impossibly deep and oh-so-icy, Kermits Pool tempts thrill-seekers who dare themselves to take the plunge for the Instagram shot of the trip. Even if that's not you, watching the adrenalin junkies

is a great spectator sport, and the cool, water-smoothed ledges around the pool allow you to sit and take in your surreal surrounds.

Kermits Pool is as far as you can explore independently in Hancock Gorge. Downstream over more tricky terrain lies Regan's Pool, named for SES volunteer James 'Jim' Regan who died here while rescuing a tourist in a flash flood in April 2004. While the route to Kermits Pool is short (1.5km return), you should allow a couple of hours to explore.

01 Are you brave (and agile) enough to take on the famed Spider Walk?

02 You'll need to negotiate deep, watery chasms on your adventure to Kermits Pool.

HANDRAIL POOL 89/100 ☐
AT WEANO GORGE

01

Dive into the hypothermic waters, if you dare.

A class-5 favourite amongst adventurous Karijini wet-walkers, this deep, emerald waterhole is so named for the shiny handrail that years of nervous, gripping hands have polished en route to Lower Weano Gorge. What begins as a gentle, moderately challenging wander (class 3), quickly turns wet and wild as you leave the rocky trail from the car park and begin to splash and scramble along rock slabs and skinny ledges.

Removing your shoes is the best way to deal with the lack of track and negotiate your way through Weano's slender, steep-sided chasm. Suddenly, the gorge dramatically opens up to reveal a stunning amphitheatre that cradles Handrail Pool between soaring rock walls. The breathtaking vista is rivalled only by the way ahead: an airy climb down the old 'handrail' and an icy plunge into the pool.

Afterwards, warm up on sun-baked rock slabs, gazing up at the tiny wedge of blue sky high above or brave the 'swim-through' beyond Handrail Pool.

A sign at the top of the gorge mentions the possibility of hypothermia, so yep, pack a fluffy towel, prepare for icy temperatures and set out early in the day to beat the crowds that often bottleneck above the final handrail.

If this class 5 scramble is not your thing, the Upper Weano trail is a grand alternative (class 4, 1km, 45mins return). Close by, catch sunrise (or sunset) from Oxer Lookout, peering into the abyss where Weano, Red, Joffre and Hancock Gorges unite.

01 What's waiting for you in lower Weano Gorge.

02 Journey to the centre of the earth on the walk in to Handrail Pool.

03 A silver handrail guides you through a corridor of slippery rocks.

JUNCTION POOL 90/100 ☐ AND OXER LOOKOUT

01

Catch sunset from the spot where four gorges unite.

If what you crave from your Karijini experience are some stellar sunset photographs, save an afternoon for the airy vistas showcased along this short, easy trail. Stop at Junction Pool lookout first for neck-craning vistas deep inside Hancock Gorge, peering 100 metres over red terraced cliffs into Junction's mystical, rarely visited pool.

01 The glorious view from Juntion Pool lookout.

Continue on over rockier ground to Oxer Lookout for startling vistas of the kings of Karijini – four flaring, red rock gorges that join forces at this spectacular spot. Cast aglow in the striking afternoon light, Weano, Hancock, Red and Joffre Gorges provide a remarkable canvas for every sunset spectacle, so pack something cold to sip and keep your phone or camera handy. The short, easy trail to Oxer Lookout (via Junction Pool) sets out from a small car park just past the Weano Day Use Area (class 3, 800m, 30mins return).

PUNURRUNHA ⁹¹/₁₀₀ ☐
(MOUNT BRUCE)

01

Catch sunrise from WA's second tallest mountain

In a region not known for its lofty peaks, Mount Bruce (Punurrunha) offers some rare altitude, elevating walkers to WA's second-highest viewpoint (it's numerically easy to remember; 1234 metres high). It takes three hours to reach the top for incongruous sweeping vistas of the magnificent Hamersley Range on one side, and the open-cut Marandoo iron mine on the other. This stellar climb is especially enchanting after winter rainfalls that trigger extravagant wildflower blooms and carpet Mount Bruce with purple mulla mullas, yellow flowering sennas (cassias) and bright northern bluebells.

01 The hike to the peak reveals scenes reminiscent of The Lion King.

Set out early to catch sunrise (armed with a head torch), following the ridge up the mountain's western flanks and keeping watch for the giant piles of tiny stones that mark the subterranean homes of the Pilbara's pebble mound mice. As you hike, honey hakeas, mulga and spinifex gradually give way to stunning Antarctic pines, and close to the summit, chains sort out the challenge of tackling some rather airy climbs. At six hours return (9km, class 5), it pays to get an early start. For a shorter walk, the Honey Hakea Track (4.6km, 3 hours), is a worthy alternative.

In case you are wondering, WA's tallest mountain is also in Karijini – it's just much harder to get to. Found in the south-east corner of the park, Mount Meharry is 1249 metres high.

HAMERSLEY GORGE ⁹²/₁₀₀ □
AND WATERFALL

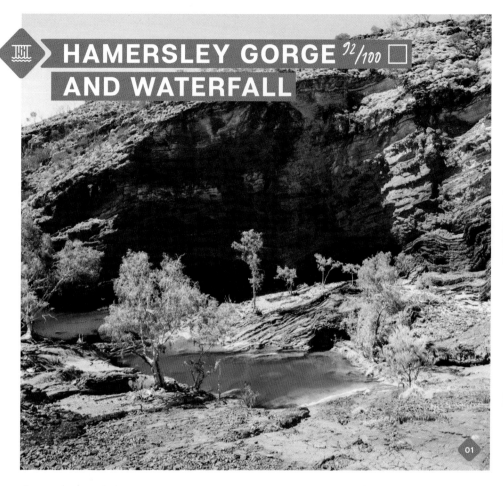

01

A geological dreamscape, set aglow at sunset.

Follow the setting sun to this much-photographed gorge in Karijini's far northwest to watch the bewitching, end-of-day play of light on Hamersley's dramatic, sheer rock canvas. Carved by Hamersley cascading falls, great contortions of richly coloured rock form a stunning backdrop to the emerald rock pools at its feet.

The sunset crowd tends to stake out Hamersley's high lookout, but arrive early and you can drop down to the water's edge to spend an afternoon cooling your heels and floating beneath the falls. Upstream you can hike to the hidden Spa Pool and be one of the few to discover the Grotto's magical fern-filled chasm.

When the sunset show ends, travellers steel themselves for the long, rugged drive back to Dales Campground or Karijini Eco Resort, but self-sufficient travellers needn't rush on. Hamersley Gorge boasts the park's only legitimate free camping area, with a toilet, picnic shelter and free solar-powered Wi-Fi.

The unsealed roads around Hamersley Gorge are razor sharp, and visitors are frequently stalled due to punctured tyres (let some air out to prevent it happening to you). Visit the gorge en route to Millstream-Chichester National Park via the unsealed Roebourne-Wittenoom Road or grab a free permit from Tom Price Visitor Centre to travel Rio Tinto's shorter, Iron Ore Rail Access Road (**tomprice.org.au/plan**).

01 Bring a pool float to explore the emerald pools of Hamersley Gorge.

02 Warm your body on the hot rockface after a chilly dip in the hidden Spa Pool.

02

SPA POOL 93/100 ☐
& THE GROTTO

An Instagram hotspot and a truly hidden gem.

It's quite possibly Karijini's smallest swimming hole yet this dazzling plunge pool is Instagram-famous and just a 10-minute scramble from Hamersley's main gorge pool. As you'd expect, the trail to Spa Pool is well-trodden and easy to follow. Just look to your right after descending the stairs from the car park and head on to the upper pool. Swimming across this waterhole is safer and easier than walking around, and from here, Spa Pool is just upstream.

Carved to circular perfection by millions of years of surging seasonal rains, swirling and eddying deep into the rock, Spa Pool's tiny stone crater is filled by a flurry of white water early in the dry season. A plunge into the icy blue pool is

de rigueur, even if you have to queue up over the winter months for your chance to slide on in. Capturing a shot beneath Spa Pool's trickling, mossy falls is worth the wait, but beware – the narrow entrance is dangerously slippery and best approached by sliding slowly in.

Unmarked and unknown, the Grotto is as secret a spot as the Spa Pool is famous. There's no signage or trail, and scant information online, making this magical, fern-fringed chasm a real hidden gem, deep and sheer and tucked into the left-hand side of the gorge up the boulder-strewn creek bed past the upper pool. Locating it is a bit of an adventure, but the solitude that awaits makes it all worthwhile.

01 Come at midday to get the pool in its best light. Come early to avoid crowds.

LEARN

They call this an ancient landscape, but Karijini's Hamersley Range really is.

Here, brightly coloured layers of iron-rich sediment contorted into magnificent designs and revealed by erosion, are a mind-boggling 2.5 billion years in the making. Indigenous Australians have called the region home for at least 20,000 years, and their stories, knowledge and culture are woven into the landscape. There is so much to learn about Karijini's past and two great ways to uncover it.

KARIJINI VISITOR CENTRE

KARIJINI EXPERIENCE

HADEAN EARTH

Close to Dales Gorge in the park's east, Karijini Visitor Centre is a cultural centre with intriguing displays that will answer all the questions you'll ponder as you explore. Designed to resemble a goanna moving across the landscape, the centre showcases the Banjima peoples' heritage, instilling in visitors stories that turn Karijini's adventure playground into sacred ground too. Drop by for maps, souvenirs and to cool down. Located on Banjima Drive, it's open from 9 am to 4 pm daily (April to November).

A five-day festival that's all about food, music, culture and history, the Karijini Experience immerses you in a culture that has called Karijini National Park home for 20,000 years. Hosted by the Indigenous Banjima peoples in April each year, the festival indulges visitors with gastronomic events like the unique bush tucker high tea, film screenings, yoga in the gorge, dreaming workshops, local art exhibitions, live music and more. For tickets and event schedules, head to **karijiniexperience.com**.

Scientists who look into the composition of earth in its earliest stages (Hadean Earth, named after the Greek god of the firey, brimstoney underworld), are fascinated by the rocks of the Pilbara. Captured in the landscape, which is 2.5 billion years old, is evidence of rock formations that are up to 4.3 billion years old, and likely part of the earth's first solid crust. So, when people describe Karijini as ancient, there's almost nowhere else on earth as deserving of the term.

KARRATHA AND THE DAMPIER ARCHIPELAGO

Flying high from wild adventures at Ningaloo Reef and Karijini National Park, visitors find themselves in a distinctly industrial scene in coastal Karratha.

A saltworks, iron ore loading facilities, one of the world's largest fertiliser plants and finally, the great flaming spires of Australia's largest liquefied natural gas plant – all of it, incongruously studding a landscape of such cultural significance and natural beauty that an eminent world heritage listing is only a matter of time.

But to discover Karratha's undeniable splendour and unearth its world-renowned Indigenous heritage, you only need to get to the water's edge. On this stretch of rugged Pilbara coastline, the Dampier Archipelago's scatter of 42 coral-fringed isles is impossibly close, accessible to boaties and kayakers who could spend weeks fishing and snorkelling, and camp in blissful isolation on beaches nestled against hills of fractured ironstone rubble etched with 35,000-year-old petroglyphs.

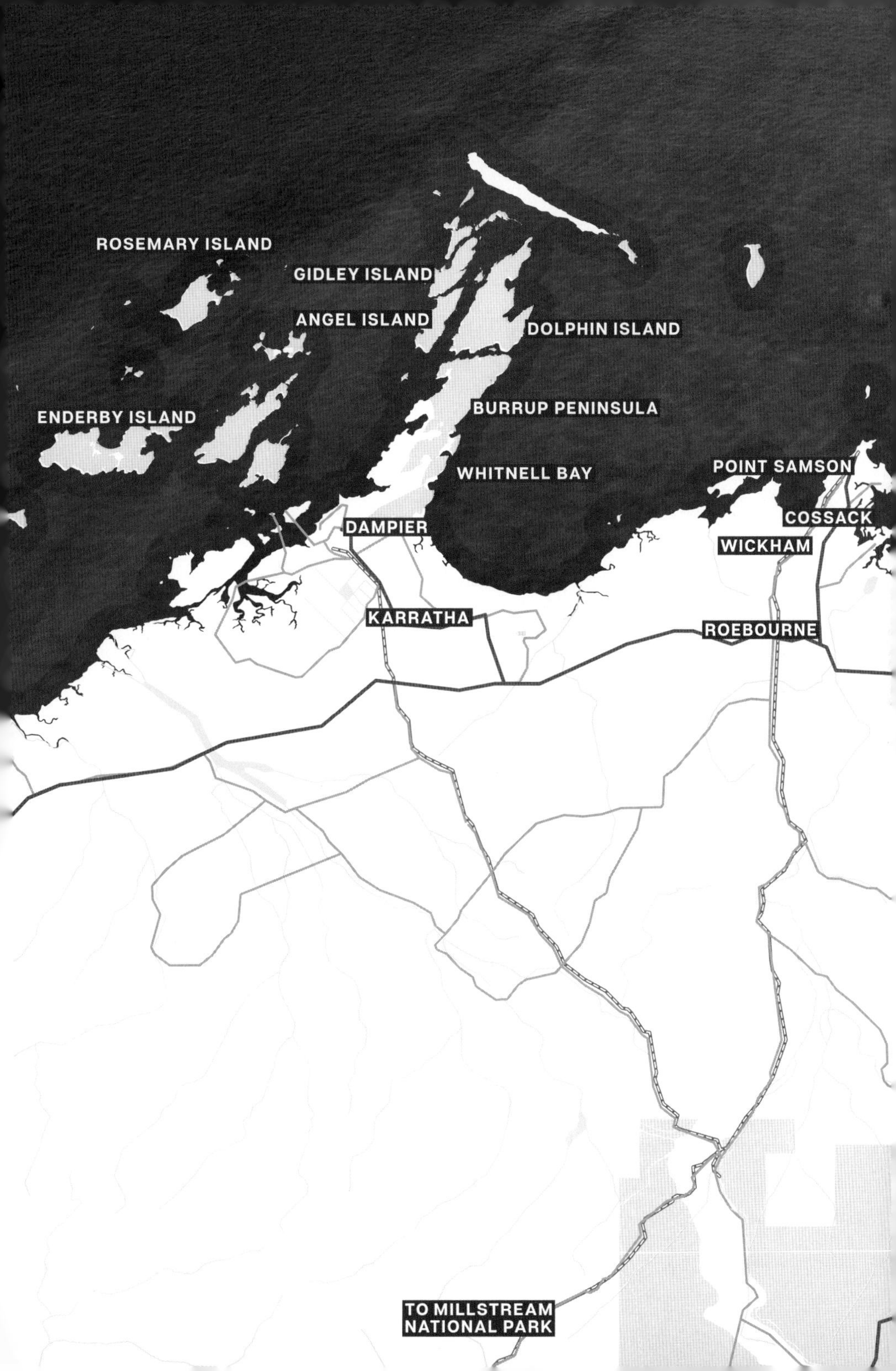

ROSEMARY ISLAND

GIDLEY ISLAND

ANGEL ISLAND

DOLPHIN ISLAND

ENDERBY ISLAND

BURRUP PENINSULA

WHITNELL BAY

POINT SAMSON

COSSACK

DAMPIER

WICKHAM

KARRATHA

ROEBOURNE

TO MILLSTREAM
NATIONAL PARK

Colourful and flavoursome, the Coral Trout is a highly prized catch.

Murujuga National Park protects the lion's share of more than a million rock engravings, recognised as the world's most extensive rock canvases of Indigenous art. Together with ceremonial and artefact sites, Murujuga's sacred sites record the long history of the Pilbara's traditional custodians, collectively known as Ngurra-ra-Ngarli, and you've never seen anything like it.

On the other side of Karratha, Cossack's pioneer-era ghost town acts as a living museum, preserving a slice of pearling and gold rush history no longer visible on the west coast. Head here to sleep inside the old police barracks (no roughing-it required), to devour a Devonshire tea on the verandah of the Customs House, and to step inside an old turtle soup factory hosting Australia's richest regional art show.

To say that this region will surprise you is a massive understatement. The fishing is out-of-this-world (think mangrove jacks and mud crabs, barramundi and bream), and the 'Staircase to the Moon' seen from Hearson Cove rivals anything you'd head to Broome for. Inland, this landscape is just as remarkable. At a sacred Indigenous oasis along the spring-fed Fortescue River, you can float, fish and paddle, hike and bike, and park your caravan or pitch a tent in the startlingly verdant Millstream Chichester National Park.

When you finally come in from the wilds, Karratha's resorts and eateries will soothe you with luxurious rooms, locally brewed boutique ales, and plenty of laidback places where you can sit and sip with sand on your feet. If you like to hike, tackle one of the Pilbara's most rugged walks – the 16km-long Chichester Range Camel Trail – or climb above Karratha to discover Indigenous rock art and petroglyphs, artefact scatters and grinding stones on the Yaburara Heritage Trail. This part of the Pilbara is so much more than just a mining town. Wait until you explore it.

STAY

Find yourself a secluded island or camp out by the beach, fishing rods ready.

Because of the fly-in, fly-out nature of the comminity up here, temporary accomodation can seem utilitarian. But venture outside of the caravan parks and bungalows, and there's some genuine class to the options available.

MACKEREL ISLANDS

Make your castaway dreams come true, and rent your own coral-fringed isle at the Mackerel Islands, scattered close to the coast off Onslow. Everything you can do in the water, you can do off the Mackerels. Thevenard Island offers all-inclusive resort stays, while Direction Island is one for wilderness escapees with a solitary, shabby-chic beach shack and all the serenity you crave. Access is via a 45-minute ferry trip out of Onslow, a seven-minute flight or aboard your own boat (it's 22km off shore) **mackerelislands.com.au**.

CLEAVERVILLE CAMPGROUND

This is beachfront living at its very best, custom-made for self-sufficient travellers who park their rigs on the edge of the sea and shake out the fishing rods. The no-frills, nature-based camp opens year-round, and it's free from October to April (three nights only) and $16 a night (or $92/week) in the peak winter months. Facilities are basic (just toilets, a natural boat ramp and a few bins), but most come here purely to fish off the mouth of Cleaverville Creek, strike a campfire and stargaze 20 minutes' drive north of Karratha, **karratha. wa.gov.au/camping**.

THE RANGES

A luxurious choice for couples (from around $250 a night), the roomy, self-contained apartments at The Ranges come with a balcony and shared pool. **therangeskarratha. com.au**
They are a fresher take on the rooms at Karratha International Hotel, which offers a livelier vibe, plus poolside dining and a fitness centre. For families, superior cabins at Discovery Parks Karratha come with all the extras that kids will love (and a price tag parents can afford). There's a swimming pool and playground, and plenty of budget-priced sites.

MILLSTREAM HOMESTEAD $^{94}/_{100}$ ☐
AND JIRNDAWURRUNHA POOL

A wild, tropical oasis that's steeped in history.

Across the thirsty Pilbara plains, this tropical oasis lures travellers to the water's edge where rare Millstream palms shade sacred, lily-covered Jirndawurrunha Pool. Poised on its banks amidst a picturesque scene, 100-year-old Millstream Homestead preserves a slice of pastoral history that stretches back to 1865, when sheep grazed these isolated wetlands and the station held the Australian record for the highest price paid for fleece.

The homestead was converted to a tavern in the mid-1970s and today serves as an interpretive centre for the Millstream Chichester National Park that protects it, chronicling the area's Indigenous history too (open daily).

Long before pastoralists arrived, the Yindjibarndi people gathered at Jirndawurrunha Pool for inter-tribal meetings and feasts taken straight from the streams. Swimming is not allowed, but a wander here is refreshing, especially at dawn and dusk when sacred kingfishers and rainbow bee-

01

tap, drinking water, picnic tables and interpretive displays to enjoy while you stir your cooking pots. There are wheelchair-accessible toilets, and generators are permitted, and sites cost $11 per adult, $7 for concession cardholders and $3 for kids.

The mighty Fortescue that flows along the park's southern edge supports an unusual ecosystem of wildlife species, well adapted to their dynamic environments. Nocturnal campers might spot endangered northern quolls and rarely seen ghost bats, and by day, dingoes, jewelled geckos or the Pilbara olive python, often found nestled in shady riverside nooks.

Included in the park's boundary but located about 50km away is the steep-sided waterhole at Python Pool. From the pool, an excellent walking trail follows the Chichester Range Camel Trail (16km/6hrs return), or a stiff trail climbs Mount Herbert for endless coastal views (600m/25 minutes return).

eaters hunt on the wing (750m/30min return). For watery fun, bike, hike, or drive to Deep Reach Pool, 9km away on the spring-fed Fortescue River, where you can fish, swim and paddle (Deep Reach, page 210). For grand vistas and a scenic tour of the national park, Snappy Gum Drive is 2WD-accessible over the dry, winter months (20km loop).

Camping is the only way to overnight in this national park, and Miliyanha Campground offers spacious bush sites and an excellent communal hub with free gas cookers, hot water on

Millstream Chichester National Park is located 165km from Hamersley Gorge via the 4WD-only Roebourne-Wittenoom Road, and 140km from Karratha and 210km from Tom Price via Rio Tinto's Iron Ore Rail Access Road (free travel permits required, available online at tomprice.org.au/plan). Park entry is $15 per vehicle. Visit from June to August. **parks.dpaw.wa.gov.au**

01 Swimming is not allowed at Jirndawurrunha due to its cultural significance to the Yindjibarndi people.

DEEP REACH POOL, 95/100 ☐
MILLSTREAM CHICHESTER
NATIONAL PARK

Wash off the red dust in this permanent waterhole.

In the shimmering Pilbara heat, mirages materialise at this deep, wide pool that revives weary travellers all year round. It's fed by an ancient aquifer along the mighty Fortescue River, and the Yindjibarndi people call it Nhanggangunha, home to Barrimurdi, the Warlu serpent of their dreaming stories.

It rates as one of the most sacred resting places on the Yindjibarndi's extensive homelands, and there's a presence here that inspires silence. Despite any urge you might have to dive in, the Yindjibarndi way is to slide in gently so as not to disturb Barrimurdi or the brilliantly coloured waterbirds that stalk the riverbanks.

The largest of the Fortescue's permanent waterholes, Deep Reach Pool is perfect for paddling, so bring

01

The best way to arrive at Deep Reach Pool is via the Red Roo Trail, a dual-use hiking and cycling trail that connects Miliyanha Campground with the waterhole, 9km away. Following an undulating path beneath snappy gums and bloodwoods high above the river, the cycling adventure takes about 45-minutes each way, or two to three hours on foot.

Another riverside wander, the shorter, interpretive Warrungunha Trail, doesn't get you all the way to Deep Reach Pool, but leads through diverse grasslands and woodlands of melaleuca and riverine vegetation to a clifftop lookout on the Fortescue River at Warrungunha (class 3, 8km, 2.5hrs return).

Time your trip from June to August when temperatures are cool, the access roads dry and wildflowers blanket the Pilbara: great carpets of fuzzy, purple mulla mulla and Sturt desert peas, bright orange cockroach bushes and sunny wattles and sennas that all soften the harsh, red dirt landscape.

a canoe, kayak or SUP to explore downstream (you can even go fishing). Broad steps provide easy river access for swimmers and paddlers launching boats, and even a shady home for the Pilbara olive python we spotted holed up underneath. However you choose to explore, you'll need to portage your boat 300 metres from the car park first. There are waterfront picnicking nooks with shady tables and wood barbecues and a toilet block at the car park.

Close to Deep Reach Pool, Stargazers campground is a basic bush camp that's ideal for solitude seekers. Generators aren't allowed, and you'll need to top up drinking water at nearby Miliyanha Campground, but there are gas barbecues and toilets, and overnight stays cost $11 per adult, $7 for concession cardholders and $3 for kids (**parks.dpaw.wa.gov.au**).

01 Slide in gently and keep an eye out for waterbirds along the riverbank.

DAMPIER 96/100 □
ARCHIPELAGO

01

Fish, snorkel and kayak through this pristine cluster of 42 coral-fringed isles.

Irresistibly close to the coast, this idyllic chain of rocky isles provides a rare, reef-fringed oasis for boaties, paddlers, anglers and divers, and the wild things that call this paradise home. Clustered in a 45km-radius from land and girthed by a marine park that protects

the richest marine biodiversity in the state, the archipelago's 42 islands and islets are dotted with 35,000-year-old Indigenous petroglyphs.

The fishing is wild, every sandy beach is perfect, and fringing coral reefs bring snorkellers and marine life rapturously together. The entire archipelago is an important turtle-nesting site, and dolphins and dugongs are routinely spotted, surfing the waves that spill into blue, coral-filled lagoons. Humpbacks are spotted here, too, on their annual northern migration from July to September.

The archipelago is within easy reach of day-tripping boaties, but if you're looking to get castaway, a kayaking adventure here is the stuff of dreams. Paddling distances are short, you can free camp for up to five nights, and there's a whopping 4500 marine species to discover, including great nurseries of sharks and rays that gather in the shallows at the southern tip of Dolphin Island.

A recommended route sets out through Flying Foam Passage to explore Dolphin Island's petroglyph-covered ironstone hills and camp on the beach. This seemingly innocuous passage bears the name of the 33-ton coastal schooner Flying Foam, which disappeared without a trace back in March 1872.

Throughout the 1880s, violent cyclones wrecked entire fleets of pearling luggers and merchant ships sheltering inside this passage, but the biggest death toll came with the grisly Flying Foam Massacre, an 1868 retaliation battle with white settlers that killed up to 150 Yaburara people.

Today, when the weather is calm, you can paddle north through the passage to Legendre Island or ride the swell to the western sides of Gidley and Angel Islands to snorkel protected lagoons and fish the oyster stacks on Angel's southern tip.

From Withnell Bay (on the mainland's Burrup Peninsula), it's a 10km run across the open waters of Mermaid Sound to explore East or West Lewis Islands, the site of one of the archipelago's earliest pastoral settlements. Or camp on the remote northern tip of the Malus Island group where whaling and pearling stations operated from 1870 to 1872.

While there's magnificence under the sea, the archipelago's sandy-fringed clusters of razor-sharp spinifex and ironstone rubble provide little shade and no facilities, so pack plenty of drinking water, snorkelling gear and reef-friendly sunscreen. If you stay overnight, bring a fuel stove and a shade shelter or tarp to keep the sun off.

Camping is permitted on Eaglehawk, Malus, Delambre, Gidley, Angel, East and West Lewis, Enderby and Dolphin Islands, and Collier Rocks, within 100m of the high-water mark for up to five nights (book at **parks.dpaw.wa.gov.au**). Boat ramps are located at Dampier (Withnell Bay), Karratha Back Beach, Johns Creek, Point Samson and Cossack. Be aware that tides flow in reverse through Flying Foam Passage, so the outgoing tide flows south towards the mainland. Visit from June to September when cool, comfortable temperatures average 13-26°C.

01 North of the Burrup Peninsula, Flying Foam Passage offers kayakers protection from the wind and swell.

MURUJUGA ⁹⁷/₁₀₀ ☐
NATIONAL PARK

Discover the world's largest Indigenous art gallery.

Chiselled into the Burrup Peninsula's fractured hills, more than a million petroglyphs record the history of the Ngarda-Ngarli; the world's largest concentration of Indigenous rock art.

Declared WA's 100th national park in 2014, Murujuga National Park protects a sizable chunk of that art around a site called Ngajarli by the Ngarda-Ngarli.

Discover great canvases of animal tracks and spiritual beings alongside long-extinct megafauna, thylacines and what is believed to be the oldest depiction of a human face. There are shell middens and fish traps, and the hills guard ancient archaeological sites: standing stones, ceremonial grounds, stone artefacts, quarries and graves.

The Ngarda-Ngarli traditional owners believe that creation spirits (Marrga) etched the rocks in Dreaming times, laying down laws and customs. The art is found right across this region, but at Ngajarli, near Dampier, a 700 metre-long boardwalk provides great access with interperative signage that gives it all meaning.

Late afternoon is the best time to explore Nganjarli or join guided tours with Experience Murujuga (1.5hrs, adults $75) and Ngurrangga Tours (2 hours, adults $95), or 4WD north to Withnell Bay to explore more of Murujuga National Park.

To reach Nagajarli, head 25km west of Karratha on Dampier Road, turn right onto Burrup Peninsula Road and right onto Hearsons Cove Road. Find out more at **parks.dpaw.wa.gov.au.**

EAT

From top-notch fish and chips to internationally inspired delicacies, the food scene in the Pilbara is not what you're expecting.

Follow food trucks around the neighbourhood or dine in community run clubs overlooking prime ocean vistas. Or settle into an arvo session of live music, local brews and exceptional Mexican. Pilbara food is awesome.

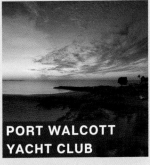

NORTH WEST BREWING CO

Team a Neap Tide pale ale with cod ceviche tostada, and you'll understand why crowds gather at this brewery for Sunday Sessions and Wednesday's all-you-can-eat tacos. Kick-start things with a Sundowner (American amber ale) or an Island Hopper (IPA), then order beef birra quesa tacos or a Greek lamb pizza teamed with a rejuvenating ginger beer. The seafood is local and there's food for vegos and kids. Open daily 11 am-10 pm; on Mooligunn Road, Karratha. Check **facebook.com/ northwestbrew**.

THE FAT BUDDA

When it's time for sunset picnics, this fiery little food truck offers an authentic, aromatic menu of Thai street food. It's run by a local called Nun, whose Bangkok-inspired dishes have locals raving (and returning). Try the basil and chilli stir-fry or the herby pad kee mao. There are spring rolls and pork balls, and if you order ahead at **hungryhub. com.au**, you won't have to wait in the queue. The truck opens for dinner (5-8.30 pm) but moves around Dampier and Karratha, so find it first on Facebook **facebook. com/fatbudda1**.

PORT WALCOTT YACHT CLUB

Chilly, club-priced brews sipped within sight of the sea as the sun disappears across Nichol Bay: perfect. It's the region's best-kept secret, tucked away on the Point Samson Peninsula, where locals love to hang out and fish. The local volunteers who run the club welcome visitors - sign in at the bar. If you're staying in Point Samson or Cossack, this is the place to come on Sundays for Fish and Chips and Sundowner nights (adults $13 and $7 for kids). Boat Beach Road, Point Samson. **facebook.com/ portwalcottyachtclub**

HEARSON COVE'S 98/100 ☐
STAIRCASE TO THE MOON

The moonrise spectacle you thought belonged to Broome.

When the tide retreats and a full moon rises over the Pilbara, a shimmering golden staircase appears at Hearson Cove, bouncing across the mudflats and climbing to meet the moon. The fleeting phenomenon appears just three nights each month coinciding with the March to October full moons. It might be best known around Broome, but you can see the staircase right along this coastline, and the shallow arc at Hearson Cove provides the perfect canvas.

When the tide returns, this stunning sandy cove is a sheltered spot to swim and picnic, bound by rugged ironstone hills on the edge of Nichol Bay. Here, explorer F.T. Gregory came ashore back in 1861 and discovered a coastline bristling with potential for the pastoralism and pearling industries.

There are barbecues, shade shelters and toilets by the beach, and if you arrive to find that the low tide has stolen back the sea, you can walk across the exposed mudflats all the way to a sandy cay where turtles nest.

In the late afternoon, when the rock art is best revealed, take a walk along the boardwalk at Ngajarli in Murujuga National Park. Afterwards, return to Hearson Cove to catch the sunset and moonrise spectacle, which is so good, it has its own full moon tour. Join guides from Ngurrangga Tours for some Indigenous-led coastal foraging, followed by Dreamtime stories and stargazing (**ngurrangga.com.au**).

If you stay in Dampier or Karratha, Hearson Cove is within easy reach, but you can also catch a good 'staircase to the moon' at Onslow (306km south of Karratha), Reader's Head at Cossack, and in Port Hedland too. Hearson Cove is located 28km from Karratha, about a 30-minute drive.

LEARN

With a history stretching back 35,000 years, there's plenty to occupy your mind in the Pilbara.

The Ngarda-Ngarli peoples' history stretches back 35,000 years and it's easy to find evidence all over. More recently, European colinisation is supurbely preserved a places like Roebourne, Cossack and Dampier.

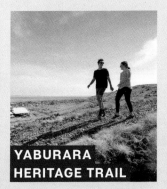

YABURARA HERITAGE TRAIL

COSSACK ART AWARDS

OLD ROEBOURNE GAOL

Rising above Karratha, a rugged hilltop lures walkers runners to an Indigenous Talu (lookout) for incredible views. Preserving the local Yaburara peoples' cultural sites, the rocky trail links petroglyph and rock art sites and reveals artefact scatters and grinding stones. There are short loops within this 5km-long network of trails, making it accessible to most walkers. After an early morning climb, refuel on organic bullet coffee and bagels served fresh at Empire 6714 on Sharpe Street, Karratha.

It's an internationally renowned art awards held in a ghost town's former turtle soup factory. For three weeks in winter, this art show literally takes over the town, filling the best of Cossack's century-old bluestone buildings with artistic works from around the country. The Cossack Art Awards is the richest acquisitive art award in regional Australia, awarding close to $50,000 in prize monies. Entry is free, but you'd best bring your credit card. **cossackartawards. com.au**

If you ended up in this 'law and order' precinct in the late 1800s, you could be arrested, sentenced and jailed without ever leaving. A police station, gaol and courthouse all in one, the Old Roebourne Gaol was a harsh spot to end up, which explains why Ellemara (the uncle of warrior Jandamarra) choose to escape and walk 950km back home to the Kimberley. Today the museum displays photos and artefacts that preserve a broader slice of the region's history and is open daily over winter. $5 entry, kids free.

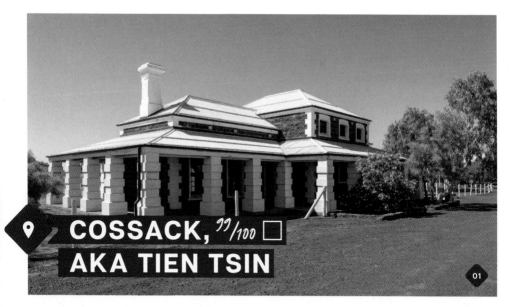

COSSACK, 99/100 ☐
AKA TIEN TSIN

01

Overnight in the most beautiful ghost town in the West.

This was the place that kick-started the Pilbara's industrial revolution, back when gold and pearls were plentiful, and the bustling, multicultural hub of Tien Tsin shipped wool to London and Mother of Pearl to Singapore. When Governor Weld himself sailed into town aboard the HMS Cossack in 1871 to gift Tien Tsin a new name, the town was a 1000-strong community of Malays, Indonesians, Chinese, Japanese, Filipinos and Ngarluma Aborigines, working together on the land and under the sea.

Progress seems unstoppable, and construction boomed: the Post and Telegraph Building in 1884, Galbraiths Store and Customs House, a courthouse, police barracks and even a

turtle soup factory. No one anticipated that the Pilbara's seemingly unlimited resources would eventually run out, but by 1900 the boom times went bust.

The gold rush was over, and overfishing of Cossack's pearling grounds sent the fleet packing to Broome. A cyclone damaged the town's wharf, and a new port at nearby Point Samson that better accommodated larger vessels sounded the death knell for the town. By 1910, the township had dissolved.

Deserted for decades, its ghostly bluestone buildings at the mouth of the Harding River are now beautifully restored, and in late 2020, the entire town was put up for sale. Just how Cossack will be reborn remains to be seen, but for now, there's plenty to do. You can bed down in the old police barracks, complete with tiny holding cells (although at $125/night, you won't have to sleep in them), or park your rig in one of four private campsites at Settlers Beach (just $15/night).

There's free entry to the Cossack Museum, and a café operates out of Customs House serving breakfast and a smashing Devonshire tea on a breezy verandah overlooking Butchers Inlet. Galbraith's Store (now the Cossack Gallery) showcases local art exhibitions year-round and sells all kinds of Indigenous-styled wearable art and homewares (free entry). The Bond Store hosts the Cossack Art Award, awarding almost $50,000 in prize monies.

Tackle the Cossack Historical Trail (6km) and turn back the clock to an era when cyclones sunk entire fleets of pearling luggers and disease and disasters tested the townsfolk.

The trail begins at the Bond Store (once a turtle soup factory), where interpretive signage guides you through the old town to Customs House, the police barracks and lock-up, the Post and Telegraph Office, and the Cossack Museum in the old courthouse (around 3km return). You can shop and eat along the way before continuing your walk to the Tien Tsin lookout, and the wharf and tram station by the sea.

The town's bricks-and-mortar might be incredibly impressive, but history is not the only thing that keeps travellers around Cossack. Catch salmon and bream from the old fishing wharf and beaches, or boat across the river to the mangrove-rich old leprosarium site to snare mangrove jack, barramundi, and mud crabs.

Walk or drive on to discover the Chinese market gardens, segregated cemetery and the Reader Head Lookout on the edge of town. or head to Settlers Beach to swim and picnic and discover the Indigenous petroglyphs on the nearby cliffs. Sandy Beach is another good swimming spot, and there are grand sunset vistas from the Reader Head lookout. Cossack is located 50km east of Karratha, signposted off the North West Coastal Highway. Visit over the cool winter months and plan your stay at **cossack.org.au**.

01 The old Courthouse is now a museum, which is free to enter.

02 Inside the historic Courthouse.

POINT SAMSON[100]/[100] ☐
AND HONEYMOON COVE

Mud crabs, mangrove jacks and magical moonrises.

If you lived in Karratha, this is where you'd escape to for long weekends full of fishing and snorkelling and boating to faraway, secluded beaches (to fish a bit more). The angling really is that good, rivalled only perhaps by snorkelling sessions along the colourful coral reefs that fringe Honeymoon Cove and Main Beach.

By day, the sandy beach at Honeymoon Cove is a beaut spot to swim and snorkel on a high tide, but return as the full moon rises to be completely wowed by Point Samson's own 'staircase to the moon'. It only takes place three days a month around the March-to-October full moons, but it's worth timing a trip around.

If fishing is your thing, launch a boat at Johns Creek Boat Harbour and poke up the tidal rivers and inlets for mud and blue swimmer crabs, prawns and prized catches of barramundi and mangrove jack. Sam's Creek Inlet is a reliable spot, as is Point Samson Reef offshore. If you haven't brought a boat, cast a line for bream off the harbour wall, or drive out to the causeway along the Roebourne/Point Samson Road to spot turtles and reel in anything from queenies to golden trevally, flathead

and bream. You might even score mangrove jacks or a barra.

Of all the long, sandy beaches surrounding Point Samson, kid-friendly Main Beach offers two kinds of fun: go swimming on a high tide, and explore the rock pools revealed when the water retreats beyond the reef. Jump one beach over to snorkel the reefy coves nestled along Back Beach (best tackled on a half-tide).

The history of Point Samson is inextricably linked to Cossack's demise, for when an unnamed cyclone all but destroyed Cossack's wharf in 1898, a deeper, more accommodating port at

Point Samson sounded the death knell for the town which was dissolved and soon-after, abandoned. After a century of cyclones, there's not much left of the original 1900-foot jetty, which finally burned down in 1991, but a lookout high above is a top whale watching lookout from July to October. For the complete history lesson, spend a few cool, early hours wandering the Point Samson Heritage Trail.

For a simple beach stay, Point Samson Resort keeps things civilised, and Samson Beach Chalets and The Cove both offer caravan and camping sites too. Samson Beach Tavern specialises in breezy sunset views and surf'n'turf dinners, and you'll find all of it at the tip of the peninsula, north of Roebourne.

01 Go swimming or snorkelling at Honeymoon Cove.

02 Watch the sun set or rise from the new Point Samson Viewing Platform.

Exploring Eden Media

100 Things to See On Australia's Coral Coast was first published in 2021 by Exploring Eden Media

ISBN: 978-0-6484646-5-5

All enquiries should be made to:

Exploring Eden Media Pty Ltd
250 Princes Highway, Bulli, NSW, 2516
publications@exploringedenmedia.com

A catalogue record for this book is available from the National Library of Australia

Contributing Authors: Melissa Connell, Catherine Lawson and Grace Hamill
Editor: Brendan Batty
Design: Matthew Ware, OBJKTIVE

Printed in Malaysia for Imago Group

The paper used in this book has been sourced from sustainable forests certified by Forest Stewardship Council® as part of our commitment to environmental responsibility. Find out more at fsc.org.

Disclaimer

Some of the activities mentioned in this book are dangerous and many of the regions are wild and remote. Consider your own safety and that of your companions when undertaking travel or participating in activities referenced within, which you undertake at your own risk. The maps contained within are soley for illustration purposes and should not be relied upon for navigation.

PICTURE CREDITS

Miquela Vos, @miquelavos; cover, cover inset, **208** | Grace Picot, @shotbygrace; inside front cover, **9, 10, 12, 147, 156, 157, 170, 184, 189, 191, 192, 194, 195, 201, 202, 204, 226** | Savio Furtado, @patsythepatrol; **4, 16** | Brook Smith @theleftlaners; **8, 113** | iStock/Lkonya; **11** | Lucia Arcadia, @oliveandmustard; **13, 29, 41, 48, 56, 57, 61, 62, 64, 65** | Todd Thimios, @toddthimios; **14, 161, 163, 164, 175** | Alex Baxter @baxterbackpacks; **19, 74** | Koh Yamaguchi, @koh.pics; **20, 32, 33** |Takuto Ishii, @yolo_heymate; **21** | Connor Sheilder, @consheid; **22** | Anna Oliver, @seachange_leeman; **23, 39** | iStock/chameleonseye; **24, 137, 167** | iStock/Dobe; **25** | Simon Maisch; **25** | David Bristow, @wildtravelstory; **26, 83, 96, 115, 118, 119, 120, 129, 130, 143, 152, 188, 190, 196, 198, 199, 200, 210, 212, 214, 222, back cover** | Melissa Pontre, @melissapontre; **27** | iStock/bennymarty; **28** | Sam Valtenbergs; **29** | Jan Kühnel, @traveldvootes; **30** | Dave Ratcliffe, @ratcliffe_dave; **31** | Philip Schubert/Shutterstock; **31, 220, 221** | Nick Dunn; **33, 95** | Anne Downing, @letmebefreeblog; **34, 35** | Calum Stirton, @calum.stirton; **35** | Mathias Sehnke, @msehnke; **36** | Illegal Tender Rum Co.; **37** | Starfish Cafe; **37** | Lobster Shack; **37** | iStock/MXW Stock; **38, 180** | Katie Brown @our.wild.unknown; **40, 108, 150, 165** | iStock/Totajla; **42** | Jemima Dobie, @gold.tones; **44** | Nathan Jarvis, @nath.jarvis; **45** | Rachael Fallon, @rachaelfallon; **45** | Joao Serafim/Shutterstock; **45** | Magdalena Grek, @magdaziuta; **46** | Abrolhos Adventures, @abrolhosadventures; **47, 70** | Belair Gardens Caravan Park; **49** | Old Pindar Hotel; **49, 65** | Faye Martin; @maxandfaye; **49, 107** | Nils Hay; **50** | Daniela Rodrigues, @dany_perth; **52, 53, 59** | Kirbie Gibson @midwestwaimages; **53, 58, 68** | Matt O'Donoghue @matt.odonoghue.images; **54** | Nikki Tremain, @travelwiththetremains; **60, 97, 98, 109, 110, 160** | Yamaji Arts Centre; **61** | Tehmi Sukhla, @tehmi; **61** | The Jaffle Shack; **63** | Totojang1977/Shutterstock; **63** | The Provincial; **63** | Oakabella Homestead; **66** | Ben Vines, @being_ben_v; **67** | iStock/Ivy Hajduk; **69** | Chris Stenger; **72** | Jake Stone; **73, 79** | Lynga Longa Station; **75** | Kalbarri Backpackers; **75** | Murchison River Caravan Park; **75** | Melissa Nicolson @melissanicolson; **76, 77** | Felicity Taylor and Kane Wells @flic_taylor @thereand_back; **78, 79, 128, 131, 140, 168** | Jay Murrin, @a_trip_overland; **80** | John Cornell; **81, 89** | iStock/Photon-Photos; **82** | Patricia Fenneteau, @diannefnt; **84** | Artur Begel/Shutterstock; **85** | Efetova Anna/Shutterstock; **85** | klaikungwon/Shutterstock; **85** | iStock/Cappan; **86** | EA Given/Shutterstock; **88, 89, 89** | Ken Griffiths/Shutterstock; **90** | Skye Morgan, @skyemarie__; **91** | Dudlajzov/Dreamstime; **92** | Kalbarri Boat Hire; **93** | Bruce Connell; **94** | Tourism Australia; **99, 124, 209, 218** | iStock/Damian Lugowski; **100** | EQRoy/Shutterstock; **101** | Lella B/Shutterstock; **101** | Shark Bay Seafront Apartments; **101** | Rory White and Emma Stievano, @emandrozdoaus; **102, 103, 171** | Tim Mitchell, @hereweareaustralia; **103** | Jackson Dye/Shutterstock; **104** | Western Woodfire Pizza, **111** | Old Pindar Hotel; **111** | Tourism Australia/Brinkley Davies; **111, 121, 125** | Benny Marty/Shutterstock; **114, 122, 123** | Tourism Australia/James Fisher; **116, 117, 126** | trabantos/Shutterstock; **127, 134** | iStock/ClaraNila; **127** | Dreamstime/SappheirosPhoto; **127** | Elizabeth Mitchell, @liz_mitch; **131** | MJTH/Shutterstock; **131** | Carly Easton, @letsgetouttahere_; **132, 151, 155** | Cynthia Burnell; **135** | YARUNIV/Shutterstock Studio; **135** | Tanawat Tintab/Shutterstock/; **135** | Gwoonwardu Mia Cultural Centre; **136** | Samantha Chin, @samantha_esther; **138, 146, 169** | Totajla/Shutterstock; **141, 142, 144, 206, 216** | Dreamstime/MarcWitte; **148** | Nicolas Yott and Shayde Love-Linay, @coupleandacar; **154** | Philipp Spatzl Fotografie/Shutterstock; **159** | Bullara Station Stay, @bullarastationstay; **159** | Tourism Australia/Sal Salis Ningaloo Reef; **159** | Lilly Palmer, @lil_palm; **162, 167, 172** | Exmouth Surf Centre, @exmouthsurfcentre; **165** | iStock/Christopher Heil; **166** | Melissa Connell, @lifeinthslowlane; **166, 186, 203** | Adrift Café, @adriftcafe_exmouth; **171** | Whalebone Brewing Co, @whalebonebrewing; **171** | Dive Ningaloo, @diveningaloo; **173, 182, 183** | iStock/terrababy; **174** | Matt Deakin/Shutterstock; **176, 207** | Emily Hamley/Shutterstock; **177** | Tom Keamy, @janthevan19; **178** | Dreamstime/Philip Schuburt; **187** | Tourism Australia/Karijini Eco Retreat; **187** | Bila Bakonyi, @adventureswithourkids; **187** | Janelle Lugge/Shutterstock; **193** | iStock/mabe123; **197** | iStock/ChristianB; **199, 205** | Wikimedia Commons/Five_Year; **205** | Karijini Experience, @karijiniexperience; **205** | Inga and Russ, @livelifenowadventures; **209** | The Ranges Karratha; **209** | North West Brewing Co.; **217** | The Fat Budda; **217** | Kings Rope Access/Shutterstock; **217** | City of Karratha; **219** | Wikimedia Commons/Yewenyi; **219** | Define Design/Shutterstock; **223** | Brian McMahon; **224**

From The Publishers

Books like this don't come together overnight, and this guide has been one of the most significant undertakings of our small publishing house. Building on the format and content of our first two guides, 100 Things To See In The Kimberley and 100 Things To See In Tropical North Queensland, we've nearly doubled the word count of each of those books, and added so much more information on the region's history and heritage, places to eat, sleep, stay and learn. We spent months on the Coral Coast in research and have reached out to inumerable businesses, locals and travellers to fill in gaps and clarify information to make sure it's as reliable as possible. We think this is the most comprehensive guide to the region ever produced.

Throughout the book we've mentioned a number of businesses and local venues. We want you to know that not a single word inside this book has been paid for by 'sponsorship'. Businesses and places mentioned were chosen purely on merit and because they come highly reccomended by the many named and unnamed contributors to this guide. If you think we've made a mistake – let us know.

Finally, we want to thank you, the reader who is exploring the Coral Coast with this guide. Books are pointless without readers, so we hope we've inspired you to look around the next corner, or over the next hill, and take in the best bits according to the locals.

Melissa Connell and Brendan Batty
exploringedenbooks.com
@exploringedenbooks